For You

Andreas Seidl

Handover of Power

European Version

Volume 6: Media

Imprint

Bibliographic information of the German National Library:
The German National Library lists this publication in the
German National Bibliography; detailed bibliographic data
are available on the Internet at http://dnb.dnb.de.

Cover: Christiane Ebrecht
Translation: DeepL, Cologne
Production and publishing: BoD – Books on Demand,
Norderstedt

ISBN: 978-3-7562-9352-0

Acknowledgements

My thanks go to my family and friends who have made me who I am today. Special thanks to all those who supported me in writing this book. I would like to thank all my classmates, teachers, fellow students, lecturers, demonstrators, activists, colleagues, companies and countries with whom I have had the privilege of sharing the experiences from which all the ideas in this book have emerged. I would like to thank the staff of Books on Demand for their kind helpfulness. I thank the citizens of Seligenstadt for the harmony and solidarity in which I was able to write.

Foreword

This policy concept contains a variety of proposals for possible political reforms. It can be peacefully and democratically adapted to any current political system of any state in the world, but also to political systems in families, clubs, associations or companies. Wherever humans make or submit to rules that manage living together, the following proposals can be helpful. Readers who find the proposals so helpful that they would like to implement them together with like-minded people can contact the author. The contact form on the last page can be used for this purpose.

Faults and defects

I ask for your understanding that this volume was not professionally proofread. I could only afford professional proofreading for the summary. Spelling errors and unfortunate phrasing may therefore occur. As soon as this volume has sold enough to pay for a professional proofreading, it will be done. After that, a new edition will be published.

English version

Please understand that this volume has been translated automatically. I could only afford a professional translation for the summary. Poor wording and spelling errors may therefore occur. In case of doubt, the German version shall prevail. As soon as this volume has sold enough to pay for a professional translation, it will be done. After that, a new edition will be published. It was more important to me that no one in the world should have an information advantage than individual translation errors in the complete work.

References
If something has been quoted directly, it is set in italics. If the headings contain footnotes, the sources for direct and indirect quotations apply in the chapter for which the heading stands. Otherwise, quotations or source references are directly at the word or at the end of the sentence or paragraph. This book contains parts of text based on the Federal Constitution of the Swiss Confederation of 18 April 1999 (as of 12 February 2017), abbreviated to BV[1] and the Constitution of the Canton of Bern of 6 June 1993 (as of 11 March 2015), abbreviated to KV[2].

If the constitutional paragraph, or individual paragraphs thereof, are based in whole or in part on extracts from the BV or KV, this is indicated in a footnote. The references to the corresponding footnotes for constitutional paragraphs are usually found after the heading of the affected chapter and sometimes in the body of the text. Articles used in the Swiss constitutions are listed in the footnote with a number after the title of the constitutional paragraph. Example: §123 Sample title: BV Art.123, KV Art.123.

All internet sources are fully cited in the footnotes. They were last accessed on 30.09.2021. All literature sources are also listed in full in the footnotes.

All references to tasks undertaken by other ministries and described in more detail there are given in footnotes. Example: Model Ministry - 1.2.3 Model Chapter.

All footnotes are to be viewed in comparison to the respective source, so-called indirect quotations. Direct quotations are set in italics, but hardly ever occur. The source reference is intended to enable further investigation and to take copyright

---

1 This is not an official publication. Only the publication by the Swiss Federal Chancellery is authoritative. https://www.fedlex.admin.ch/eli/cc/1999/404/de On 14.12.2021
2 This is not an official publication. The Bernese Official Collection of Laws is authoritative. https://www.belex.sites.be.ch/frontend/versions/2420?locale=de#ART71 On 16.12.2021

into account.

All keywords used, based on the names of the responsible units, departments and ministries of Germany, are listed at the end of this volume in the chapter on the conversion of ministries.

Table of contents

1 Goals of the Ministry of Media Affairs

As a mediative state power, the Ministry of Media Affairs aims to mediate between citizens and politicians or state employees and to find tools to manage this mediation (moderation), for example with certain television formats. The reporting, which is up-to-date in terms of content and technology, as well as citizens' opportunities for co-determination should be available digitally and via multimedia. All necessary broadcasts are broadcast in real time and all broadcasts are stored in the media directory[1] permanently accessible to all citizens.

The objective of the Ministry of Media Affairs is considered achieved when the population is fully informed, involved and educated and can exercise its control function.

2 Departments

The departments are divided into sub-departments and enumerations are usually considered as their individual units. Many tasks of some departments are completely taken over by other ministries as a service.

2.1 Central Department

Part of the Central Department is the Reception Office with the Courier and Mail Room, which directs all concerns, broadcasts and visitors to the appropriate place in the ministry.

2.1.1 Staff

The Human Resources Department is responsible for staff development and planning. For this purpose, it takes care of the recruitment of junior staff, intern and trainee programmes as well as the selection procedures for employees and special selection procedures for applicants with disabilities. For politicians and employees, the department prepares a job plan. In all its tasks, it works in voting with the personnel board.[2] All other personnel matters are transferred to the respective

---

1 Ministry of Digital - 12 Directories
2 Ministry of State Organisation - 2.1.1.1 Personnel board

ministries. The Ministry of Education is responsible for the training and further education of employees for the state service.[3] The Ministry of Labour takes over the service law.[4] This includes labour and collective bargaining law for employees in the state service, remuneration, personnel administration of all careers and employees, flexitime, holiday and sick leave, working time with or without flexitime in part-time or full-time at the place of work or in home work. The Ministry of Infrastructure provides housing assistance for all state employees.[5] The Ministry of Finance's Pay Office takes care of employees' salary, expenses, travel and relocation costs.[6] The Ministry of Education provides childcare for all employees in the state service.[7]

The Ministry of Health is responsible for the occupational health service.[8] It ensures occupational health management, deals with the treatment, education and prevention of occupational accidents, controls and provides occupational health and safety through the health auditors[9] of the Company Auditing Agency[10] .

2.1.1.1 Video casting

The personnel of the Ministry of Media Affairs are democratically elected, at least those who select content or present it on camera. The intendants of the five state TV channels, like other politicians in the election of persons process, are elected directly by the people.

Moderators, actors, reporters and authors are elected by the audience. If they are elected for a single project, a new election takes place for each new project. If they are permanently employed, a quorum of 60% triggers the new election. They

3 Ministry of Education - 2.1.1.1 Education and training for the state service
4 Ministry of Labour - 4 State enterprises, 13 Labour Directory
5 Ministry of Infrastructure - 2.1.1.1 Housing assistance for state service employees
6 Ministry of Finance - 2.1.1.1 Staff remuneration
7 Ministry of Education - 2.1.1.2 Childcare for state service employees
8 Ministry of Health - 2.1.1.1 Occupational Health Service
9 Ministry of Labour - 20.7.2 Health auditor
10 Ministry of Labor - 20 Company Auditing Agency

apply to the audience with a video of themselves or their project. The audience votes on it continuously. The most popular persons are invited to a show and compete against each other until they cooperate or are eliminated. Concepts can unify the participants during the show. Viewers decide who or what they like best.

The video casting takes place in the Media Directory and in a Government Television show. In total, the video casting lasts 4 weeks, with the show taking place on the last day of this period. Beforehand, applicants can create videos that users can rate and comment on.

In this way, the persons who work in front of and behind the camera are determined by the people. For this purpose, on the profile page of every state broadcaster in the Media Directory, there is a "Personnel Selection" section with vacancies as well as video applications for these vacancies sorted by broadcaster or format.

The aim is to find entertaining personalities who are able to communicate politics all the time, because they can also be funny and are happy to act. The task of all moderators is to be able to formulate political facts in an understandable way and to moderate discussion rounds. Moderators at municipal level are called local moderators. All moderators are employed by the Ministry of Media Affairs, except for Federal Moderators, who are employed by the Ministry of State Organisation.[11]

2.1.2 Organisation

The ministries of media, security, justice, finance, labour, state organisation provide audit services for quality management in the ministry, evaluation of work performance, revenues and expenditures, as well as corruption prevention, sabotage protection and, if necessary, disciplinary matters.[12]

The Ministry of Labour regulates procurement law and ensures corruption-free state orders and procurement.[13] The

---

11 Ministry of State Organisation - 4.4 Federal Moderator's Office
12 Ministries of Media, Security, Justice, Finance, State Organisation - 2.1.2.1 Audit services
13 Ministry of Labour - 6 Procurement Office

Ministry of Finance organises the annual budget vote and ensures proper accounting in each ministry.[14] It regulates budget procedures, budget law, staff budgets, departmental budgets, costs and cash management, and assists ministries in budget planning for the budget vote. The language service for translating talks or texts is provided by the Ministry of Education.[15]

The Ministry of Digital Affairs supports the supply of Information Technology.[16] In voting with the Procurement Office of the Ministry of Labour, it takes care of the procurement, provision, maintenance and service of technical devices and software. Much of this is produced in-house to ensure data protection in information and communication technology. Information technology and digitalisation officers audit and advise the ministries. Digital appointment calendar and documentation services are provided as well as a digital policy archive including a library.

2.1.2.1 Audit services

The audit services of the Ministry of Media Affairs are the state TV channels, in particular the Surveillance Television. The Government Television is used by those entitled to vote to scrutinise the work of government and, where appropriate, to participate directly in it. The Party Television is used to audit the plans and measures for the implementation of the laws in the ministries. The Surveillance Television is specifically for the comprehensive audit of all government activities and conducts unannounced controls and undercover investigations. The Educational Television allows citizens to audit what and how is taught in state educational institutions and what is researched in research institutions. The Youth Television also enables minors to understand the facts in such a way that they can learn about and audit the state system.

---

14 Ministry of Finance - 8 state revenues, 9 state expenditure
15 Ministry of Education - 2.1.3 Language Service
16 Ministry of Digital Affairs - 2.1.2.1.1 Supply of Information Technology

2.2 Management Department

The Management Department is the minister's department. With his office team, he provides policy planning and analysis for his ministry and coordinates the relationship between the nation and the municipality through exchanges with his deputies in the municipalities. He initiates cooperation with other ministries or citizens in committees and is supported by the Ministry of State Organisation.
The Ministry of Digital Affairs is responsible for digital management and thus provides departmental management. It automatically produces business statistics, staff surveys and the current state of research through statistics. It automatically forwards proposals to the affected or empowered state employees. In document management, it ensures digitalisation and that ministries share forms with each other.[17]

2.2.2.1 Medial service

The Party Television handles public relations for all ministries. At the request of the respective minister, it creates or reviews press releases, images, videos, speeches and texts for the ministries and publishes them on all desired state and private media channels. Party Television moderators are professionally trained to be the minister's spokespersons at press conferences or to present civic dialogue, conferences and events in a telegenic manner.

2.3 European Department

The Ministry of Foreign Affairs ensures the constant transmission of the latest information on current European policy affecting the ministry concerned, applicable European Union law and all European Union funding programmes starting or in progress.[18] The European Department ensures international networking with state broadcasters from European Union Member States in order to support domestic

17 Ministry of Digital Affairs - 2.1.2.1 Digital Service
18 Ministry of Foreign Affairs - 2.4 European Department

broadcasting authorities with information material or to jointly organise interactive broadcasts with the affected peoples.
The European Department decides for the audiovisual and media sectors[19] whether to adopt, adapt or reject existing European Union law.[20]

2.4 Department for Private and State Media Law

The Department for Private and State Media Law oversees compliance with the general rules for private and state media broadcasters or press organs. It is responsible for the general operating regulations of state broadcasting authorities and ensures the interactive participation of those entitled to vote. In cooperation with the Ministry of Digital Affairs, it operates the Format Directory and the Media Directory and orders the programming of algorithms and interactive or simulative applications on behalf of the respective editorial staff. It collects the audience ratings of all state broadcasting authorities. In voting with the Minister of Media, broadcasts with low audience ratings can be degraded.

2.5 Department of State Broadcasting authorities

The Department of State Broadcasting oversees the operation of the state broadcasting authorities and coordinates their cooperation with each other. It regulates all operating regulations that affect only one broadcasting authority at a time and are different in all others. In particular, when broadcasting authorities seek cooperation with other ministries or companies, the department is their contact. The same applies to ministries and companies that wish to cooperate with the state broadcasting.
In voting with the media minister, the formats of news, documentaries, feature films and shows of all broadcasters are evaluated for their suitability. If necessary, responsibilities are

---

19https://eur-lex.europa.eu/summary/chapter/audiovisual_and_media.html?root_default=SUM_1_CODED=05
20Ministry of Foreign Affairs - 6.4 Conversion of political contents to the policy of dynamic media democracy

reallocated between the broadcasters.

3 Tasks of the Ministry of Media Affairs

The ministry's tasks are to inform and educate the people and to enable all those entitled to vote to have a say in the state system. The Ministry of Media Affairs is responsible for ensuring the free formation of will and the undistorted casting of votes. In particular, the Ministry of Media Affairs cooperates with the ministries of state organisation and digital affairs when legislating or distributing responsibilities, so that citizens are granted their political rights.

In cooperation with the Ministry of Education and in voting with the Ministries of Digital, Innovation, Labour and Economy, all educational content is defined and made available as basic knowledge for all citizens through the state media.

It is the task of the Ministry of Media Affairs to set media law, to determine what freedom of the press state and private media have and how formats of the media are marketed. With state broadcasting, the Ministry of Media Affairs fulfils the task of providing citizens with a broad range of multimedia and interactive content. To this end, it operates the Media Directory and 8 TV channels. The Media Directory is used as an archive and virtual production platform for all state broadcasting authorities. In cooperation with the Ministry of Digital Affairs, it enables viewer participation so that they can have a say in the content of the broadcasts.

The state TV channels fulfil different tasks, which are specified by the constitution and the media minister. Government Television represents all procedures of state management in which policy is set and politicians are elected. In all its broadcasts, those entitled to vote are involved through the People's Computer[21] . News Television informs citizens about the past, present and future state of politics, the economy, culture and crime. Local Television takes federalism into account and fulfils the task of the Government Television at the municipal level. The citizens complement the programme with their regional Citizen Television. Party Television presents

21 Ministry of Digital Affairs - 13.6 People's Computers

the opinions of the parties and the work in the ministries. Nationwide Citizen Television has no requirements and serves as a free civic press. Surveillance Television fulfils the task of documenting the control of all state organs by video, so that the people can monitor the control of the state organs. Responsible persons are held accountable by the people in interactive formats and faults in the system are corrected. Educational Television performs the task of filming Tax-funded knowledge from state education and research institutions. Learners, teachers and researchers are involved in the production processes. Youth Television fulfils the task of making the content of the other state broadcasters more comprehensible for those entitled to vote from the age of ten and to promote their mental, physical and sexual development through suitable interactive formats.

4 Media law[22]

Media law splits the free and state press. Free press are private print media, publishing houses, news agencies, radio, television and the internet. Censorship of the free press is prohibited. State press is administered by the Ministry of Media Affairs and is beholden to the people and their laws. This can have implications of censorship because the state press organs are supposed to perform different tasks. For the free press, editorial secrecy applies; for the state press, elected politicians or the people can demand disclosure of an editorial board's investigation and source work.

4.1 Freedom of the press[23]

The free press enables citizens to hear a state-independent opinion as well as education, cultural development and entertainment. Freedom of the press enables the free press to decide for themselves what they will and will not report on or how they will shape their programme. The same applies to all free media that are not necessarily journalistically active.

22§15 Freedom of the media: BV Art.17
23§209 Press: BV Art. 93

Complaints about the programmes of free media can be reported to the police if a criminal offence is suspected. For other complaints, independent media can have a complaints office set up by their association. Consumers are entitled to the usual consumer protection rights.[24]

Freedom of the press ends where the rights of the individual and the people begin. The rights of the individual in relation to the press are the right to anonymity and to be forgotten. Anyone who does not expose himself or herself to the public, willingly, may not have his or her name or image reported on unless he or she gives his or her written consent.

It is the people's right to have the truth reported to them. Wherever it is not or cannot be reported objectively, this must be made clear. If there are a variety of views, opinions, research results or habits, all must be named equally or omitted. Companies in the press or reporters must make their political orientation known. This enables consumers to classify the views and to know whether they are being informed in a biased way or whether they are being presented with opposing views in a balanced way.

4.2 Formats

There is a multitude of formats for conveying content to humans and new ones are being developed all the time. State broadcasters use this variety of formats to make politics look good. TV shows present and moderate decision-making in committees or legislative processes. Feature films film party programmes, election manifestos and legislative proposals. Documentaries serve to control the power of offices, authorities and politicians. Series prepare the news from world affairs, such as economics, politics, crime or culture.

---

24 Ministry of Labour - 17 Consumer protection

4.2.1 Formats Protection Agency

All formats broadcast by the Ministry of Media Affairs are automatically protected via the Formats Protection Agency. For this purpose, the Ministry of Media Affairs cooperates with the Ministry of Innovation .[25]

If citizens or employees of the Ministry of Media Affairs and its broadcasters have ideas for new formats, they can communicate them to the Formats Protection Agency. To do this, the new format must be written in a uniform style. Once the profile for the new format has been completed, a digital check is made to see if there is already a comparable format in the world. The FRAPA database[26] serves as the basis for the search. If it is a new format, it is protected and published in the Format Directory.

4.2.2 Format Directory

In the Format Directory, profiles are created for all formats broadcast on state television that are protected by the Patent Office. Citizens can access all profiles via the People's Computer and rate formats and leave comments with suggestions for improvement. Should a format be marketed worldwide in the free market economy, the suggestions for improvement will be remunerated individually, depending on how strongly they are applied.

All profiles receive groups in which all media broadcasters and broadcasters who have already broadcast the format are members.

5 State broadcasting[27]

The Ministry of Media Affairs operates 8 broadcasters for television and radio, which perform 5 tasks. Therefore, there are five broadcasting authorities, each as an independent broadcaster. Each broadcasting authority is divided into television and radio.

---

25 Ministry of Innovation - 7.3 Patent Office
26 https://www.frapa.org/
27 §41.4 Exercise of political rights, §208.1a-e State media, §46.5 State,

Government broadcasting is responsible for reporting on decision-making by politicians on how to formulate treaties, instructions or laws. It allows viewers to participate interactively via their People's Computers for the purposes of questioning or voting. Final votes on international treaties or laws, however, must be voted on by the people during an election week. To keep the population up to date with the latest news around the clock, the government broadcasting operates a news channel. In order to better reach the municipalities, the government broadcasting, in cooperation with the local population, operates a regional broadcaster in each voluntary municipality or within an alliance of municipalities.

Party broadcasting reports from ministries and their offices and agencies. The visits of the film teams are announced and prepared together with the affected ministry. Commissioned productions are possible. The activities of all ministries are to be presented in this way. In order that citizens can also present their activities, or commission film productions, the party broadcaster operates an additional broadcaster for citizens.

Surveillance broadcasting reports unannounced and covertly from ministries and their offices and agencies. Its employees are accompanied by other state control bodies and the free press in order to gain unrestricted and legally secure admission.

Educational broadcasting presents all education content taught at state educational institutions. Much of its content is co-produced in cooperation with schools, colleges and scientific institutes.

Youth broadcasting presents the content of the other four broadcasting stations in a way that is suitable for children, summarises it and develops its own content in cooperation with minors.

5.1 Broadcasting[28]

The Ministry of Media Affairs serves to provide citizens with admission to information on how ministries operate and broadcast formats such as shows, feature films, documentaries,

---

§113.2 Media democracy
28 §208 State media: BV Art. 93

promotional videos and news to engage citizens in the processes for legislation and the election of persons.[29]

The state broadcasters produce contributions in all appropriate formats to make politics more understandable and appealing. The intranet as is used as a common media archive and platform for cooperation. Most of the state television productions are co-productions with the citizens and the ministries. This is done either in the broadcasters' studios or distributed throughout the country using the broadcasters' fleet of vehicles. The council buildings also serve as studios to ensure the publicity of government negotiations and to give citizens the right to speak.[30]

The broadcaster can be influenced by those entitled to vote by electing and deselecting staff, or by a majority demanding certain content or having it produced and broadcast by themselves.

There are 18 broadcasting centres, one in each capital city of a ministry. All state broadcasting authorities share broadcasting centres and film studios to share equipment.

State broadcasting is financed by taxes, advertising revenue and paid film productions for companies from the Barter Economy, Planned Economy and Social Market Economy for their own use.

5.2 Audience ratings

All audience ratings of all state and private broadcasters are published in the Government Television. Every viewer is asked by People's Computer if they want to participate in the ratings measurement. If the television set is also from the People's Innovation Company[31] Intranet[32] , the data is automatically sent to the Ministry of Media Affairs and is stored on the viewer's People's Computer in the Media Directory. If audience ratings are low, surveys are conducted among viewers via the Media Directory on how the broadcast should be changed or

29 Ministry of State Organisation - 9.10 Legislation, 9.9 Election of persons
30 Ministry of State Organisation - 8.4.1 Capital city and field offices
31 Ministry of Innovation - 10 People's Innovation Company
32 Ministry of Digital Affairs - 13 People's Innovation Company Intranet

whether it should be degraded.

5.3 Advertising

Each ministry and party wing is entitled to have its own advertisements produced by the Party Television and broadcast on the appropriate state television. Ministries advertise laws, parties advertise persons and their programmes.[33]
Promotional videos are produced by Party Television and broadcast on the agreed state broadcaster at the agreed time. Production costs are capped at the same amount for all parties and ministries. The broadcast itself costs nothing and must be broadcast by all broadcasters except the Surveillance Television and Youth Television. The broadcasting time is equally distributed among all ministries and parties.
Commercials for companies can be broadcast on state television for a fee, but cannot be produced. Exceptions are inventors with invention profiles in the Ideas Directory[34] and Party Economy companies who submit their promotional video applications to the Ministry of Media Affairs through the Ministry of Planned Economy, provided the promotional video is to be produced by the Party Television. Videos produced in-house are uploaded to the Media Directory on the Ministry of Media Affairs site. Planned Economy companies are Experimental Enterprises and Innovation Enterprises that are given airtime by the Ministry of Planned Economy.
All broadcasters, except the Surveillance Television and Youth Television, run advertising to cover costs in order to keep the tax share of funding as low as possible. There may never be more than 1/5 advertising in the programme. Party broadcasting is allowed to run any kind of advertising, government and education broadcasting are only allowed to run certain advertisements.
The government's broadcasting service runs advertisements by political parties, labour unions, associations for legislative initiatives and election programmes. Each party is allocated the same number of advertising minutes.

---

33 Ministry of State Organisation - 9.3.2 Election advertising
34 Ministry of Innovation - 9.4 Promotional video

Educational broadcasting places advertisements for educational programmes of international and national universities, adult education centres or public schools. Private and state education and research institutions as well as educational travel companies can advertise for customers or employees. Youth broadcasting has no advertising, but knowledge contributions from the school career between and during a broadcast. Commercial breaks are geared to the average attention span of the target group. For example, they interrupt the broadcast with advertising after 45 minutes when the target group is 14 years old.

5.4 Beta channel

Every state broadcaster has a beta channel. If broadcasts of events take place in real time and these events last longer than scheduled, the Beta channel is used. Then the broadcasts continue according to the programme schedule in the Alpha channel and the broadcast in real time continues in the Beta channel. This beta channel otherwise shows pre-produced footage by citizens, the transmission of which is interrupted.

5.5 Teletext

The teletext is there to show production information and programme content in summary form. It also displays QR codes that can be scanned by the People's Computer camera to join in the broadcast. Teletext can also be accessed via the Media Directory.

5.6 Media Directory

In the Media Directory, all broadcasts are filed in the group of the respective broadcaster responsible for the production. Broadcasts are given their own profiles there, which can be sorted by various headings, such as date, ministry, genre or format. The Media Directory is the state media library for nationals and at the same time the archive of the national broadcasters.

In each profile of a broadcast, the most recent broadcast is shown on the start page and next to it are all the interactive functions, such as contributions, comments and ratings. Below that, all past broadcasts are listed.

In the Party Television Citizens' Television Group, users can upload their own videos, have them commented on and rated. The Media Directory offers a link to the groups of state radio and TV channels. This should make it possible for voluntary film producers to be allowed to lend out the old technology of the state television stations and be trained in handling it to produce their own broadcasts.

5.6.1 Categorisation

All contributions of media content categorise the users who upload them. This happens automatically when you create a new profile. Media content is divided into audio contributions, video contributions and computer programmes.

Audio contributions go into the music, radio plays or news category and are sorted there into music styles, genres or sections.

Video contributions are placed in the category news, documentary, show or feature film. News items are sorted into the appropriate category, i.e. politics, economy, society, culture, sport. It should also be indicated whether the news is good or bad. Documentaries are placed in the appropriate area of accountability of one or more of the 18 ministries. For feature films, the length is recorded and a distinction is made between short film, long film or series. They are assigned to genres, such as comedy or thriller. Shows are assigned to their appropriate genre, such as talk, quiz or game show.

Computer programmes come under the category of games, electronic processing of data, operating systems or applications.

5.6.2 Editing programme

In the Media Directory there is an editing programme for pictures, animations, film and sound recordings. This programme runs on servers of the Ministry of Media Affairs and can access media files from the Media Directory and, if the user wishes, also on his or her People's Computer. In the programme there is also an instructional video on how to create and combine different picture settings with the camera, how to take down the sound or how to set lights. With the help of an example video, the user can watch and imitate the operation of the programme to make the video appealing and understandable.

5.6.3 Algogram (algorithm & television programme)

The Media Directory offers the function of compiling one's personal television programme by means of an algorithm. For this purpose, all the user's interests and activities on the intranet are searched. These virtual decision criteria are displayed to the user and he or she can remove ticks or specify additional interests by keyword. A weighting of the individual interests is also possible.
It is possible to use the algogram for the contributions of one broadcaster or for several broadcasters. However, this does not apply to private broadcasters. Video contributions from the Knowledge Directory can also be included in the algogram.
Another function in the algogram is to sort all contributions by ministry, so that one can inform oneself exclusively about the work of this one ministry.

5.7 Interactivity[35]

Interactivity is a central component of all broadcasters. This allows citizens to exercise their political rights to have a say in governance. The Ministry of Digital Affairs provides the hardware and the Ministry of Media Affairs produces a variety

---

35§43,2,3 Political rights: KV Art.29, §41,4 Exercise of political rights: BV Art.39, §84,4 Political civil rights

of content. Where political events are held by ministries, parties or citizens, state broadcasting authorities broadcast in real time so that any number of viewers can participate.

State television can be received via any standard television set. However, the interactive functions are only possible via People's Computer. In the teletext, the link to the broadcast is displayed in a QR code on the intranet and recognised by the People's Computer via camera. After that, you can rate all broadcasts, have your audience ratings counted and take part in interactive broadcasts. This function is provided via the People's Computer as a control panel.

In real-time broadcasts, viewers can press a button after a statement came from a filmed politician that they liked or disliked. The more citizens do this, the more the politician knows what the citizens want.

Interactivity is ensured by the following tools, among others, which can be used for all appropriate broadcasts.

5.7.1 On the scene

In order to be able to travel to the places of action in a television studio, the studio is built like a hemisphere. On the white walls, projectors create an image of the location of the action that was recorded there with a 360° camera. This allows people to talk about the surroundings in the room. Depending on the topic, this can also be a flyover with a drone over a certain terrain, which was recorded with a 360° camera.

5.7.2 Mobile Show

The mobile show acts as a mobile lobby in the political processes. Wherever state policy is at work, interests need to be listened to in order to balance them and not to hurt them. A mobile show can be used in a company or a state educational institution, for example. Affected parties align their interests with each other on the spot. For example, politicians from the government, party members from the opposition, lobbyists in favour and against, scientists and the audience. Not all of these groups and not always the same number of guests have to be on stage at every visit.

The mobile show is located in a specific place where those affected by state policy can be found. The audience is, for example, affected employees, customers, patients or clients. This audience is given voting rights and can vote on opinions, ways of working or needs in order to agree on measures that can be adopted by a majority. Proposals from those affected can be submitted to the editorial team in advance.

5.7.3 Vox Pop Box[36]

Old telephone boxes are transformed into Vox Pop boxes. Vox Pop comes from Latin and means "people's vote" (Vox Populi). The mini-studios have a camera, a microphone and a touch screen instead of a telephone. These boxes are permanently located in cities in well-visited public places and can be used day and night to record vox pops. In smaller towns, the Vox Pop boxes are located in the town hall next to the intranet café. In the box, people can be asked questions to which they respond, or they can make a statement on a topic themselves. If a new topic is to be opened, the user must enter a reference in a ministry via the touch screen in the intranet, or sort the topic into a subject area using keywords. All broadcasts can set questions that can be shown in the next broadcast. The touch screen can be used to operate the camera, edit the film and link the content to the appropriate broadcasts, ministries, subject areas, directories or profiles and groups.

5.7.4 Online Reporter

A voluntary reporter makes a video of an event and comments on it via an online switching conversation. The reporter speaks for about as long as his video of the event lasts and thus produces a background text for his video at the same time.

36§41.2 Exercise of political rights: BV Art.39

5.7.5 Voting

The easiest way to register your vote is to use the People's Computer. Usually, people should bring their own People's Computer to the event. This makes multiple voting and manipulation almost impossible. If voting via People's Computer is not possible, there are two ways to still be able to guarantee all voting possibilities.
For studio shows, remote controls are issued and for outdoor shows with unpredictable audiences, 3 tickets per person are issued. For the remote control and for the cards, the person must hand over their identity card as a deposit. This ensures that voting cannot be done twice via the person's own People's Computer.
The remote controls work with a radio signal. The cards are scanned by cameras housed in a device. This camera device is installed on a tripod on stage, set at the eye level of the largest audience member and not obscured by the podium guests.
On its top, the device has several rotating lights, similar to the blue light on ambulances, indicating majorities in the audience. As soon as a quorum of dissent in the audience or the audience with People's Computer is met, the respective light comes on. The colour scheme is based on the "Solution Finder" format concept.

5.7.6 Secret voting

In all broadcasts where voting is requested, viewers can opt for a secret ballot. If someone wavers with their hands up, the voting is made secret. Depending on the locality, this is possible in different ways.
When the show is produced in a studio, remote controls are handed out to the audience. During voting, the remotes are supposed to be turned over while pressing the button. To do this, the numbers on the buttons of the remotes can be felt. During the voting, the voting options are displayed with numbers on screens in the studio.
When the show is produced outdoors, tickets are issued to the audience. These cards have different colours, numbers and

QR codes on the front and back. During a voting, these cards are held up and scanned. During a secret ballot, voting does not begin until all guests have lowered their heads and closed their eyes. A beep will sound, at which time all guests will hold up their cards with the matching side facing the front of the stage, where the device with cameras for voting is located. As soon as the second beep sounds, the voting is over.

Viewers participating in the voting via People's Computer are asked to make their input covertly.

5.7.7 Why questions to the audience

During a show, the panel or the moderator can ask questions to the audience that cannot be answered yes or no, or give out work assignments. Groups should be formed in the audience to conduct the show. The moderator decides the size. Usually it depends on the number of audience members. Each working group meets in a certain corner of the studio or square. Depending on which work task participants would like to do or what justification they have for a question, they move to the appropriate place. Groups of 5 form at this place. After the round of introductions, the orders are to be completed or the question is to be discussed with arguments. At the end of the discussion or decision-making, a spokesperson of the group is elected who can present the results well. From these spokespersons, groups of 5 are formed again and share their results. Each group again elects a spokesperson to go on stage to present the results of their working group. The panel now makes proposals on how different camps should be reconciled or whether there should be separate solutions for each camp. The group speakers remain on stage until all questions to the audience have been clarified. As soon as the speakers do not speak in the spirit of their group, the participants in his or her group are allowed to raise their hands. If there are too many, the camera device reports this and activates the blue light so that the moderator can intervene and ask questions. Those who have raised their hands can speak at the audience microphone.

5.7.8 Audience microphone

The audience microphone is handed to the person who raises their hand and extends their finger by an assistant. There is a button on the handle that says "SPEAK". When the button is pressed, the red lamp above it lights up. The director now gets a signal and gives a signal to the moderator. As soon as the moderator has announced the speech, the control room switches on the microphone and the red lamp lights up green. As soon as it is clear that there are no more questions from the panel to the audience member or that the audience member still wants to give an answer, the microphone is switched off again. The red lamp lights up again and the assistant takes the microphone back until the next person reports comes forward. The maximum speaking time will be announced in the respective show.

5.8 Entertainment

To create a good mood in the audience so that they are engaged, entertaining elements are included in the programme.

5.8.1 Popcorn bike

There will be popcorn for the audience if enough volunteers from the audience join in. An exercise bike is used to generate electricity that powers a popcorn machine. Audience members can sit on it and watch the show. Whether they cycle only until their bag gets full or keep going for others is up to each person.

5.8.2 Break game

During the commercial break in live programmes, the moderator does an improvised play with the audience. The moderator first gives an acting action, then asks for volunteers and lets them rehearse once. After the commercial, the audience watches the performance.

6 Radio

The state radio stations are there to convert information from the state TV channels into audio-only signals. The formats used by the radio are news programmes, discussion circles, radio plays, commentaries by participants, reporters or citizens, or interviews by reporters with participants or citizens. Participants are all persons who are directly involved in the subject matter.

There is a radio station for each national TV channel and a regional radio station for each regional TV channel. Each of these radio stations has two frequencies. The first frequency is used by the state, the second frequency by citizens.

Whether citizens submit music, radio plays, news or other formats is up to them. All content submitted must be free of commercial rights. The radio stations are responsible for playing the submissions of music requests, audio books or other audio formats in the order in which the citizens have voted in the profile of the radio station in the Media Directory. The second regional frequency range is made free for citizens' events if they are registered. These can be, for example, discussion groups, music orchestras, concerts or open aerobics. The national radio stations can be received throughout the country. Because there are 5 state TV channels that can be received nationwide, there are also 5 radio stations with two frequencies.

There is also a radio broadcaster that only broadcasts music and has as many frequencies as there are music genres. There is a frequency for each music genre, such as classical, rock, pop, techno, folk music, etc., which is only played by songs and playlists of the listeners. Songs that are paid for are only played if advertising is placed in front of them and if advertising partners can be found who want to use the song as an advertising platform. Since the listeners vote on the playlist themselves in the Media Directory, the advertising can also be perceived as annoying and the paid song is dispensed with. If no advertising partner can be found, the paid song is automatically dispensed with.

6.1 Open Aerobics

Open Aerobics is an outdoor event for physical exercise. Participants move together to the same music. A radio station and all voluntary participants bring headphones and pocket radios or download the appropriate radio app on their smartphones. In city squares, this event is offered as a flash mob or regular training event.

7 Government Television[37]

Government Television is the medium through which ministries and political parties can consult with citizens. It supports citizens in exercising their political rights. The right to information and participation is guaranteed by Government Television. The Ministry of Digital Affairs is responsible for digital participation and provides the necessary computer programmes and presentation on the intranet. Government decisions can be made by politicians, councils and the people. All three forms are accompanied by the Government Television through its reporting and viewers can participate through their People's Computer.

If politicians make their decision on their own, they have to justify their decision in an interview with Government Television. In the Government Television report, affected employees of the relevant ministry also have their say. Viewers can negotiate and vote on the decision in a committee through a veto quorum.[38]

When a council is convened, the council building of the capital city of the affected ministry is used as a studio. The council meets there and its meetings are broadcast in real time on Government Television or, in the case of overlength, on the Beta channel. During the broadcast, viewers can participate through their People's Computers, but this is for statistical purposes only. What viewers can do at any time is cast their vote for the relevant veto quorum, which means that it is no longer the Council that is responsible, but a committee.

If a committee is convened, the Government Television will

37§41,2,4 Exercise of political rights: BV Art.39, §72,6 Right of initiative and petition, §107,1c Powers of governments
38Ministry of State Organisation - 9.6 Committee, 9.5.14 Veto quorum

send a People's Motor Vehicle to the public place where the committee is to be held. The place is determined by the affected ministry. Committees are implemented through the media as per the requirements of the Ministry of State Organisation.[39] The events are broadcast in real time on the Government Television or Beta channel in case of overlength and published in the Media Directory. Viewers can participate in the committee through their People's Computers.

If a legislative initiative, Counter-template or Counter-draft is introduced by a citizen, party or council, it is filmed by the Government Television, broadcast and stored in the Media Directory. The initiator takes the lead in working with the Government Television director.

When a politician is newly elected, Government Television accompanies the election of persons. It reports on the election campaign, films the election programmes of the party wings and organises the committees for programme combination and candidate selection.[40]

7.1 Equipment

Government Television has a broadcasting centre in each capital city of a ministry. The plenary hall of the council buildings is used as a studio for the council meetings. If deputy ministers are not present in person, they are videoed in. Each broadcasting centre has a fleet of vehicles. The Government Television fleet consists of minibuses for camera crews, People's Motor Vehicles and trucks with trailers for camera cranes, studios, large mobile screens and tent domes. The equipment can be lent out by other state broadcasters.

7.1.1 People's Motor Vehicle

The People's Motor Vehicle is a mobile television studio in two different versions. The small version is used for citizens' committees, the large version for People's Committees. The

---

39 Ministry of State Organisation - 9.6.3.7 Media implementation
40 Ministry of State Organisation - 9.9 Election of persons

studio consists of a partially glazed container. Cameras are mounted on the wall facing the cab and on the ceiling. The glass of the container walls can be switched from transparent to opaque and coloured luminous pixels can be displayed on it. Such glass is installed in all People's Motor Vehicles. In this way, the studios can immediately become screens for the inside and the outside. For the inside, the writing is mirror-inverted. Loudspeakers are mounted on the outside of the containers.

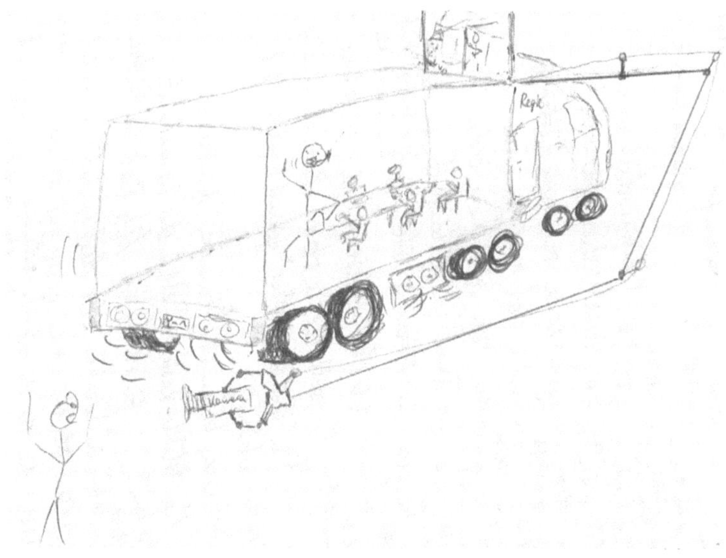

The small version consists of a standard truck tractor with a trailer for a 40-foot container. Two 20-foot containers are loaded onto it. In the front 20-foot container, close to the driver's cab, is the technology for the camera cranes and the control room for editing and data transmission via satellite or mobile phone masts. When the truck is in motion, the audience microphones including stands are stowed in the control room. The rear 20-foot container is a glass box with an oval table inside, surrounded by rotating stools. The furniture can be folded into the floor.

The large version consists of three trucks and trailers. One of them is a fully glazed 40-foot container with a table and chairs that can be lowered into the floor to create a straight surface. In the second trailer is a large screen that extends to provide space for the picture mixers in the control room. Camera cranes are mounted on this trailer. In the third trailer is a tent roof. The tent roof is a circular, flat helium balloon that inflates into a dome. Four beamers hang in the upper tip, displaying the broadcast image from every point of the compass in the dome. Provided the sun is shining at the time of the committee, the opaque tent roof is used. The four stands hold the dome roof in place in the wind and are filled with water until they are heavy enough. The TV boxes are set up in the empty tent roof container. The Truck trailers are positioned around the crowd to ensure sound coverage from all sides.

7.2 Programme[41]

In the Government Television programme are committees that affect the whole country, i.e. People's Committees, Peoples Committees or Citizens Committees of nationally affected citizens. The same applies to corresponding council meetings and ministers' decisions. Between the broadcasts there are election advertisements by parties and interest groups. In the evenings and at night there are feature films in the programme about future laws or election programmes of the parties. The formulation of new laws and the combination of programmes is done with the help of a television show with the format "Solution Finder". The proposed solution that comes out at the end of the show is put to the people or affected citizens for voting. The committee to select candidates is held in the format of "candidates' committee".

During an election week, there is comprehensive reporting on the contents of the upcoming voting. Committee summaries, explanations and animations explaining laws sentence by sentence and election programmes section by section are run. The voting results of the voting computers may only be announced at the end of an election week; interim results or polls are not permitted.

---

41 §113,3a,6 Media democracy

7.2.1 News

The news programmes on Government Television vary in length. Sometimes they are staged by Government Television and produced with its own contributions. Sometimes broadcasts are produced because negotiations by politicians have to be conducted in public. For example, negotiations on international treaties, talks with lobbyists or council meetings are filmed in real time by Government Television and broadcast on the Beta channel if they are overlong. These recordings are neither edited nor commented on by Government Television spokespersons.

7.2.1.1 Newsreel

In the Government Television there is a weekly news programme called Wochenschau. The current policy developments of all ministries are presented there. This concerns, among other things, government decisions, legislative processes or upcoming elections of persons. As soon as there is a demonstration, there will be real-time coverage as a special programme with the format "Demo TV". A summary of the demonstration is shown in the newsreel. At the end of the newsreel, the format "Crowdfunding of the Week" runs.

7.2.1.2 Demo TV

The Government Television reports demonstrations with 1000 or more registered participants in real time with a People's Motor Vehicle. The registration of a demonstration must be made via the town hall, which automatically communicates the data to the Government Television, News Television and Local Television. The Government Television arrives at the demonstration with a mobile studio, accompanies the demonstration procession with music that the organisers can submit in advance and invites demonstrators to the mobile studio for discussion after the rally. The aim is to find out what was being demonstrated against or for. Should a spontaneous unannounced demonstration occur, the nearest

People's Motor Vehicle will be dispatched as soon as possible. Should a counter-demonstration take place, the "Solution Finder" format will be used to mediate between the two demonstrations.

7.2.1.3 Lobby documentary

All talks between politicians and lobbyists must be broadcast on state television. There is a studio in the council building for this purpose, where talks with lobbyists must be held. During the legislative process in a committee, the lobbyists are invited to the panel. All discussions are saved as a documentary video and can be accessed in the Media Directory. Before laws are put to the vote, all videos of the talks held with lobbyists in the course of this law are edited together. In this way, those entitled to vote can understand to what extent special interests have been taken into account to a greater or lesser extent.

7.2.1.4 Crowdfunding of the week

From all new entries in the Ideas Directory, which present their idea profile in the crowdfunding platform[42] to search for investors and collaborators, the most popular ones are selected. The editorial team searches through all active crowdfunding projects. They compare the newest crowdfunding projects, the ones with the best rating, the ones that are growing the fastest, the ones that are about to reach the amount of money or the number of employees or suppliers, or the crowdfunding projects that are about to end. The editorial team evaluates the results for all seven categories and presents the videos and the creators in the broadcast.

7.2.2 Feature films

Government Television produces feature films to package current politically significant events in stories. The actors should enable voters to identify with them in order to recreate

42Ministry of Innovation - 8.3 Crowdfunding Platform

a state of affairs that is to become reality in the future.

7.2.2.1 Election programme filming

Party wings prepare programmes before elections of persons with which they compete against each other. Each of these election programmes is filmed by Government Television so that voters have a decision-making tool for the pre-election. The directors translate the election programme into a screenplay in cooperation with the respective party wing. Representations of the party wing can be present during the direction and lodge an appeal in case of suspected misinterpretations. Otherwise, the implementation is left to the director.

7.2.2.2 Law filming

The Government Television films laws on its own and in cooperation with the parties or with citizens who are initiators of legislative initiatives. It votes on how templates for laws are meant and how they could be interpreted. The initiators tell the directors how they are meant. If ministers are the initiators, they communicate their ideal idea of how the law will play out. The opposition, in the form of the other wings of the party, in turn describes the effects. The directors take both into account, but are not bound by instructions. In case of doubt, the intendant of Government Television is liable as a directly elected politician and the director with his deselection quorum. Doubts arise especially when the project is not presented in a balanced way but in a one-sided good or bad way. The film of each law is deposited as a link in the Law Directory.[43] The filming of the law must be completed by the beginning of the election week so that voters have a decision-making aid.

---

43 Ministry of Justice - 4.7 Law Directory

7.2.2.3 Focus films

These feature films are produced and broadcast in combination with a documentary or a show. News topics that have had and will have a long run are declared focus topics by the media minister. Focus weeks run through the entire Government Television programme for one week. Focus weeks occur up to 4 times a year. Focus feature films are to show personal experiences of main characters that persons affected by a news topic have experienced in such or such a similar way. Focus feature films become series with episodes and seasons if the topic is likely to occupy the news for a longer period of time.

7.2.3 Shows

The shows on Government Television are meant to give citizens the opportunity to become part of the government and the state apparatus, if they want to participate. In most cases, the People's Computer is needed as a tool for this.

7.2.3.1 Election of persons committees[44]

Since the election of persons can be carried out in three ways, in direct and indirect democracy those entitled to vote are the citizens. In representative democracy, those deputy ministers are entitled to vote as the council of ministers and form the audience. In the municipal election of persons with representative democracy, those entitled to vote are the members of the municipal party council and form the audience. Those entitled to vote in representative democracy are not the audience. The shows of direct and indirect democracy are conducted with a mobile studio in public places. The show of representative democracy is conducted in the plenary hall of the council building in the capital city of the affected ministry.

44§94 Digital participation in committees, §61.3 Election of persons process

7.2.3.2 Programme committee

The programme committee combines the most popular 3 programmes and 10 programme items from the pre-election.[45] The stars, plus and minus points awarded by the voters are also used. This committee is a coalition negotiation between all party wings and their programmes. The panel includes all party wing leaders whose party wing has put out a programme that is in the top 3 most popular in the pre-election. If the programme has been prepared by an individual without a party wing affiliation, that person is invited to the panel. Ministry staff are in the audience and may be invited to the panel by the moderator. They are available to answer questions on implementation. The show format "Solution Finder" will be used, but the initial voting will be replaced by the pre-election. At the beginning, all 3 programmes and 10 programme items are presented as a short video. Afterwards, suitable programme items are combined in one programme and unsuitable ones are separated in another programme. As a result, a maximum of 3 programmes are to be brought into the run-off election. Depending on how well the programmes can be combined, only two programmes or only one programme will be put into the run-off election.

7.2.3.3 Candidates' committee

The candidates' committee nominates the candidates for the run-off election.[46] There can be several candidates' committees if there are too many applicants. Up to 10 candidates can be selected in one committee. If there are more than 10 applicants for a post, there will be several candidates' committees consisting of the first round of the show format only. The show format consists of three rounds.

In the first round, each candidate introduces him/herself. Within 2 minutes, the candidate has to describe his/her CV, especially studies and work experience, name the programme he/she is running for and why he/she should be the best for

---

45 Ministry of State Organisation - 9.9.4.6 Programme committee
46 Ministry of State Organisation - 9.9.4.8 Candidates' Committee

its implementation. A video or pictures can be shown as support. However, the candidate should speak freely. During the presentation, the spectators and the audience can give their ratings in real time. After all candidates have introduced themselves, there is a line-up of all candidates and each has 10 seconds to introduce themselves again briefly. During this time, all those entitled to vote can give their remaining ratings. The most popular 10 applicants from the first round move on to the next round. In the second round, simulation games are used to simulate everyday political life in this post under the new programme and to incorporate a challenging situation, such as a boom, a decline in the birth rate or a natural disaster. In the simulation games, the candidates have to work together or make decisions alone, possibly against others. During and after the simulation game, the candidates can be rated again.[47] The most popular 5 candidates move on to the next round. In this final round, the moderator asks the candidates quiz questions, but they are why questions and do not involve pure memorisation as in usual quiz shows. Each candidate has a button in front of them and whoever presses it first gets to answer the question first. The audience and the viewers are then allowed to choose another candidate who has to answer the question. During and after this final round, ratings are given one last time.

The 2 most popular candidates for a programme are put forward for the run-off election. If more than one programme has emerged from the pre-election, the process is repeated for each additional programme. If a candidate is standing for more than one programme, he/she does not have to present him/herself for the second programme, but must justify why he/she is standing for more than one programme during the presentation time.

7.2.3.4 Wing battle

This show serves to reconcile differences of opinion and different approaches with the people. At party congresses, the different party wings decide on their programmes. A programme can

---

47Ministry of State Organisation - 9.9.4.8.2 Simulation games

be in conflict with a programme of the same party, only in a different wing. Or it can be in conflict with programmes of other parties in order to balance interests. For example, in the education party, one wing might stand for frontal teaching and grades and another wing for democratic group work. These two programmes differ within the Education Party. However, if either tax money is to be spent on building a new school or on building a new town hall, programmes from the Ministry of Education and the Ministry of State Organisation get in the way. These problems are sent to the editors by So-called conflict reports from the parties, companies, families or research institutions, or investigated by reporters. Guests are then invited to the studio for the problems and a solution is found, according to the show concept "Solution Finder".

The representatives of the different parties or party wings wrestle on stage to find a compromise, which the majority of the audience and spectators rate well. As soon as the majority solution has been found, the next problem comes up.

The show for wing wars can also give rise to counter-proposals that can be introduced into a matching ongoing legislative process.[48]

7.2.3.5 Solution Finder (Legislation Committee)[49]

This show is primarily used to draft, amend or abolish legislative texts together with citizens in a legislative committee. The ministries of media, state organisation and digital affairs are always involved in the implementation of a committee. The ministry in whose subject area a law is to be introduced takes the lead.

The concept behind the show "Solution Finder" is suitable for significantly more problem solving. Therefore, the people can apply the implementation of this show concept to any problem of their election. A worked-out show concept is available for the show format "Solution Finder", including a 45-minute pilot show, website layout and trailers as DVD.

---

48 Ministry of State Organisation - 9.10.4 Counter-proposal
49 §94 Digital participation in committees

7.2.3.5.1 Aims of the show

The Ministry of Media Affairs provides its viewers with a platform that enables them to solve public problems that they could not solve on their own. The state thus gives its citizens the opportunity to turn bad situations into good ones. For politicians, one goal is to get as many viewers as possible to participate in decision-making so that there are stable majorities. The higher the audience ratings, the more certain it is that the bill will find the necessary majority in the election week.

At the beginning there is the decision which proposals will be discussed. At the end there is the decision which solutions will be sent. During the discussion there is always the possibility of different solutions. The discussion group in the studio consists of moderators, experts and the audience. If it wants to ask for the opinion of the masses, there is a short interruption for an opinion poll of the viewers at the TV sets and People's Computers.

To keep viewers excited about the next broadcasts, they will be given the opportunity to influence the next two episodes immediately after an episode by voting on the show's profile page in the Media Directory.

7.2.3.5.2 Regularisations

The rules of discussion are that nothing and no one is criticised, only suggestions for improvement may be expressed. All participants state or deposit their names, especially if it is a digital participation, to avoid multiple voting or manipulation.

7.2.3.5.3 Experts

The experts are the affected politicians from the affected ministry, scientists from state educational institutions, stakeholders from the affected associations and affected citizens. They are requested in advance of the event at the request of the responsible minister and invited to the panel. Experts must testify truthfully and if they do not know something, they must state this clearly.

7.2.3.5.4 Moderators[50]

There are three moderators, one for the panel (M1), one for the audience (M2) and one for the voting (M3).

M1 moderates the experts, looks for solutions in their statements, writes them down and combines them into sentences. He asks for the experts' opinions on whether this solution is feasible or what could make it feasible. He asks for the opinion of the audience, whether they like this solution or whether someone has a better idea. In case of doubt, the opinion of all audience members decides between two alternatives and removes one of the solutions from the discussion. M1 finds ways to reach consensus between experts, audience and spectators who participate through their People's Computer.

M2 moderates the audience, goes to the guests who raise their hands, asks for the idea and the name, introduces the guest, keeps the microphone in his hand, touches the shoulder of the guest who talks too long, takes the microphone away from the mouth if the guest does not stop talking or says something other than an idea for improvement. M2 reads the anonymously submitted ideas aloud. M2 engages the audience and the panel in a dialogue to improve the solution just discussed.

M3 moderates the audience, writes key terms, recommendations, proposals voiced on the panel in concise words on the screen, shows the voting on the screen, activates the voting periods and presents the results. M3 is the moderator who captures opinions, packages them into understandable language, displays the results in percentages, and is responsible for counting the votes cast. M3 brings opinions and majorities into the discussion through a screen in the studio. The screen is located above the heads of the panelists and is so large that even the guest in the last row of the audience can still read what is written there.

All moderators communicate through light. All five lights are displayed on a device that is placed on the central table where M1 is sitting.

Blue = Idea: M2 activates it when someone in the audience has an idea

Green = Approval: M3 activates it when more than 50% raise the green card

---

50 §94.6 Digital participation in committees

Red = Rejection: M3 activates it when more than 50% raise the red card
Yellow = Chatter: M3 activates it when more than 30% in the audience raise both hands
White = Opinion: M1 activates it when there are two competing solutions in the discussion M3 activates it when more than 50% in the audience hold the red card on top or when the majority is unclear between red and green cards.

7.2.3.5.5 Co-determination for spectators[51]

Viewers on the television and in the audience have various opportunities to participate. Viewers who want to participate via their People's Computer must first register on the show's profile page in the Media Directory with one click. This way, no one can vote twice. The issue poll is replaced by a quorum that triggers the committee, or the minister or council with their drafts and counter-proposals.[52]

7.2.3.5.5.1 Favourite idea

With the favourite idea, users should find the best idea. They can make a proposal on how the problem could be solved. To do this, they enter the proposal in a list. The earlier they do this, the more time other users have to read and rate the proposal. There are 100 characters available for a solution suggestion. Or users can choose an existing proposal from one of the other users and vote for it. One day before the next episode is recorded or broadcast in real time, this voting ends. The inventor of the most popular idea is invited to the studio and sits in the front row of the audience. During the week, you can see if your proposal is at the top by clicking on "popularity" instead of "date" in "sort".
The favourite idea can also be recorded and uploaded as a video message in the Vox Pop Boxes.

51§94,4,5 Digital participation in committees
52Ministry of State Organisation - 9.6.3.2 Convocation

7.2.3.5.5.2 Broadcast

To be able to participate during the broadcast, you have to log in on the profile page of the show. This is possible via a link, which is shown as a QR code in the teletext. You have to scan this QR code with the People's Computer and you are immediately on the profile page of the show. Now you have to click on "log in" to be part of the show and on "log out" if you don't follow the show any further because you have switched off the TV or changed the programme. This is important in order to be able to determine the number of all viewers, which shows the turnout as a percentage of those entitled to vote. Citizens attending the event in person will receive personalised voting cards in red and green if they do not have their People's Computer with them.

7.2.3.5.5.3 Order

Before the discussion, people vote on the order in which the proposed solutions should be discussed. The five proposed solutions are the favourite idea from the website and one proposal from each of the four experts. The results of the audience vote flow together with the results from the website. The result is the order in which the proposals are gradually developed into majority solutions until the broadcasting time is over. This does not apply to legislative proposals in committees. Here, all the proposed solutions are discussed to the end for which the viewers and audience have decided. The show continues on the Government Television Beta channel.

7.2.3.5.5.4 Audience idea

While a proposal is being discussed, any guest in the audience can raise their hand to call for M2. M2 will introduce the guest and have them speak into the microphone. If the idea is to be voiced anonymously, M2 will hand out paper and pen, collect it back and read the idea aloud. Audience members use their control panel on the People's Computer. The blue button opens a text field with 150 characters. Users can immediately see and rate these proposals in a side window like a chat history. Positively rated proposals are taken up by M3 and introduced into the discussion. For queries, the viewer can be called via the People's Computer by video telephony. Computers are distributed in the front row of the audience. This is used to continuously search for ideas during the solution discussion, block spammers and contribute useful ideas by report. M2 then activates the blue light and reads out the idea or M3 activates video telephony in case of queries to the author.

7.2.3.5.5.5 Chatter

If a person in the studio talks too long without contributing a proposal for a solution, the audience should raise both hands until the person stops talking. There is a yellow button on the control panel that says "chatter". This button must be held for as long as the chatter lasts. If more than 50% of the users hold the button down at the same time, M3 gets a signal on his PC and activates the yellow light.

7.2.3.5.5.6 Doesn't work! Doesn't exist!

Persons who only say why a solution does not work are shown the sign by M1 with the inscription "Doesn't work! Doesn't exist!". If they don't have a better idea, they have to be quiet. The inscription "Doesn't work! Doesn't exist!" is on a button in the control panel and when 30% of the audience presses it, a siren sounds briefly in the studio and moderator M1 raises the sign saying "Doesn't work! Doesn't exist!". Then, if the speaker doesn't have a better idea, he has to be quiet.

7.2.3.5.5.7 Live support

Audience members receive a green and a red voting card. If they think a statement is bad, they raise the red card for five seconds. They lift the green card for the same amount of time if they like the statement. There are two buttons next to each other in the control panel. The red button can be used to express spontaneous disagreement with a statement, the green button to express agreement. This support is displayed on a screen in the studio as a diagram and fluctuates like a stock market price. As soon as 50% disapproval is reached, a short warning signal sounds.

7.2.3.5.5.8 Opinion poll

Anyone in the audience who does not like a solution raises the red card and keeps it up as long as the solution is being discussed. As soon as more than 50% of the audience guests and spectators do this, M3 activates the opinion poll. Then two alternatives have to be formulated by the panel, either with "yes or no" or with "either or". The audience then decides with the voting cards. There is a white button marked "Opinion". This has to be held down as long as people talk about the unpopular way of finding a solution. If more than 50% of the registered users hold the button down, a news item appears on M3's PC. M3 then activates the white light and carries out the voting.
In the opinion poll, a question or two statements are displayed in the People's Computer. Here, a tick must be placed either at "Yes" or "No" or behind the "Either" or the "Or" statement that one agrees with.

7.2.3.5.5.9 Final vote

All proposed solutions from the discussion that are ready to be voted on are written on the list for the final voting. Each solution can only be voted on with yes or no. Solutions with a majority of more than 50% are put to the voting. The audience and viewers decide whether to approve or reject each proposal. The list of all proposed solutions or legislative texts discussed in the broadcast is displayed in the control panel. One can now accept or reject each proposal individually. This allows one or more templates to be put to a vote. Templates that exclude another template are included in the voting as a Counter-template.

7.2.3.5.5.10 Live broadcast

It depends on the transmission speed of the TV channel, the TV sets and the intranet speed for the People's Computers whether breaks are needed during a live broadcast. Live broadcasts can have a delay of up to 5 minutes due to technical circumstances during transmission. During the breaks, music is played and advertisements are shown on the television.

7.2.3.5.6 Run-through

In this exemplary run-through, the cooperation of the participants and the time schedule become clear. The following abbreviations are used. M1 corresponds to the moderator for the panel, M2 to the moderator for the audience, M3 to the moderator for the voting, E1 to E4 to the experts on the panel and G to speaking guests from the audience or spectators.

7.2.3.5.6.1 Info block

Three moderators come into the studio and welcome the viewers. M1 announces the topic and presents the news overview. During 5 minutes, excerpts from news programmes and magazines are shown on the screen. M2 presents the sitcom. In the sitcom, M3 and M1 perform an improvised play on stage that illustrates the problem. M2 moderates the on-site report. M1 and E1 explain in the recorded on-site report where they are and what the expert's job is, which has as much to do with the problem as possible.

7.2.3.5.6.2 Voting on the order

M1 welcomes the experts to the studio. All the experts say their proposal. The winner of the favourite idea says his proposal. M3 opens the first voting. The audience votes by remote control and audience members vote by People's Computer. M3 closes the voting and announces the order in which the proposals will be discussed. In this example, E1's idea has come in first place.

7.2.3.5.6.3 Solution discussion

When the moderators address or involve the audience, they always mean the audience guests in the studio and the viewers with People's Computers.
M1 asks expert E1 to briefly explain his proposal. M1 asks the other experts whether this proposal is feasible. Each expert either says how the proposal could still be implemented or why it is not implementable and how it could be implemented instead. M3 asks the audience to express agreement or

disagreement whether they like what the experts have proposed or not. They can do this while the experts are talking, or when all the experts have spoken, M3 asks the audience. The experts should try to get as little disagreement and more agreement as possible, thus fulfilling the will of the audience. In case of doubt, an opinion poll is taken, moderated by M3 and voted by the audience.

Here, for example, the alternative of E2 loses and the alternative of E3 wins. When someone talks just to summarise something, more and more people in the audience raise both hands or audience members press the yellow button "chatter". That person then stops chattering or is interrupted by M3. When a person in the studio says that something can't be done, M1 shows the sign that says "Doesn't work! Doesn't exist!". This person asks the others for help. Especially in such situations where the experts run out of ideas, the audience comes into play. If a guest from the audience has an idea, he reports and M2 takes care of him. M3 immediately opens a post on the show's profile page in the Media Directory and displays it on the screens in the studio. This way, all the experts can check all the incoming proposals at the same time and take them up if necessary. Once a proposal is feasible, there is a discussion about who needs to implement the proposal to make it work. Now the search for the appropriate addressee or addressees begins, following the same discussion pattern.

Not every solution to a problem has to become a law, but if a ministry is designated as the addressee, it can become a law. M3 writes down the finished first proposal and M1 asks E2 to briefly explain his second-placed proposal. The following parts of the discussion are the same as above.

7.2.3.5.6.4 Final vote

M3 opens the final vote with all the solutions found in this episode. The audience can reject or accept each solution individually. M3 presents the solutions with a majority of over 50% and prepares the letters with the solutions to be sent or handed out to the appropriate addressees. These can be experts on the panel, for example if a minister is one of the four experts. If the proposals are legislative proposals that will result in a referendum, the majority for this proposal must correspond to 70% of all participating audience guests and viewers.

7.2.3.5.7 Implementation alternatives

The sitcom can also be performed by a theatre ensemble. The play is recorded on stage by a nearby theatre. The recording is broadcast on Info Block.
How many experts are invited is up to the problem. Two is the minimum to reflect views. It depends on the size of the problem and how many areas should be covered. Four is balanced and small, but larger rounds are also possible.
Audience members could also bring their People's Computers and dispense with the voting cards.
The Solution Finder Show can be used with a People's Motor Vehicle in a wide variety of locations.

7.2.3.5.7.1 Demonstrations

In the case of demonstrations, the responsible town hall reports the organisers' registration data to the Ministry of Media Affairs. If the expected number of participants is high, a mobile studio is sent to the demonstration. The demonstrators are the audience, the organisers, knowledgeable professionals and politicians from parties and ministries are the experts on the panel. The show takes place after the final rally of the demonstration. Here it becomes clear whether the audience votes differently from the spectators. This can be an indication for the demonstrators whether they represent a majority opinion or a minority opinion.

7.2.3.5.7.2 Company

It is also possible to solve problems of companies. In this case, Government Television only provides the infrastructure, hardware, software and perhaps the moderators and experts for the show. Most of the experts should come from the company itself. This method is possible at general meetings or during labour disputes. Planned Economy and Social Market Economy companies can request the show free of charge. Free Market Economy companies can request it for a fee. Broadcasting on state television only happens if the companies agree.

7.2.3.5.7.3 Everywhere

Whenever many people come together and have problems, whether with each other or whether everyone suffers from them, the Solution Finder concept can be used. It can be used free of charge as a PC programme, or at Government Television the necessary infrastructure can be rented for a fee. The rental costs are only waived if the problem has relevance for society as a whole and 10% of the citizens agree to use tax money for the production of a broadcast.

Just as the people can call a committee by veto quorum, at least 500,000 persons can also order a show in solution-finder format by People's Computer or signature list at the Town Hall. This can be done on the show's profile page in the Media Directory.

Those who want to use the format for themselves without a TV recording can download a programme from the show's profile page in the Media Directory. This programme makes one the organiser of the solution finding. All participants involved are selected by the organiser from the directories on the intranet and invited. The solution finding can be done either face to face or fully or partially through the Intranet and the People's Computer. Experts can also be consulted.

7.2.3.6 People's Plenum

As soon as a People's Plenum[53] is used for legislative processes of representative democracy, a plenary hall is set up in a stadium on the field. All the deputy ministers of a Council of Ministers take their seats there. The plenary debate on an emerging law is conducted here with a larger audience and real-time transmission. The opportunities for audience participation are the same as in the show "Solution Finder". Speakers are broadcast to screens and stadium speakers. The audience uses their People's Computers for co-determination. After a speech, the audience can clap as much and as loud as they want. Several measuring devices measure the volume as feedback.

53 Ministry of State Organisation - 9.6.2.5 People's Plenum

7.2.3.7 Consultations

This show shows the negotiation of international treaties, whether with companies, or within the framework of an International Union[54], or intergovernmental treaties with third countries.[55] All negotiation rounds are broadcast unabridged in real time and then saved in the Media Directory.

In the first round of negotiations, the participants say what they want to negotiate and what they do not want to negotiate. After the first round of negotiations, the consultation phase begins, during which questionnaires can be filled out by citizens. The citizens decide in the questionnaire to what extent they are willing to negotiate or not about the things mentioned. Here, hard and soft limits are set on how far the negotiation can go. Soft limits can be sacrificed for compromise, hard limits cannot.

At the beginning of the consultation phase, the questionnaires are presented in the show, what is behind the questions and what are the implications behind different answer options. The Minister of Foreign Affairs and the responsible staff members are in the studio to answer questions from the audience. At the end of the consultation phase, there is another broadcast in which a volunteer fills in his questionnaire publicly in the studio. Once the volunteer has completed his or her questionnaire, the consultation phase ends. During the broadcast, automatic evaluations of the questionnaires are made and the foreign minister interprets the first results. The second round of negotiations will follow in the next broadcast. During all negotiation rounds, the current number of votes for the veto quorum for this negotiation is displayed at the bottom of the screen. As soon as this quorum is met, a committee is convened and the show "Solution Finder" takes over the broadcast. If the citizens remain in agreement with the negotiations, only the treaty is voted on in a people's vote.

---

54 Ministry of Foreign Affairs - 5.8 International Union
55 Ministry of Foreign Affairs - 5.5 Consultations

7.2.3.8 Phanta Philo Sofa

With the Phanta Philo Sofa, ethics committees[56] are prepared, which are then broadcast in a show format on the Government Television that the Ministry of State Organisation prescribes. On the Philosofa, the focus is on philosophising about states and how they could be explained. The Phantasofa is about fantasising about the future and how a state might play out in the future. In this show, two different sofas are placed side by side on stage. The moderator sits on a swivel chair in the middle between the two sofas.

7.2.3.8.1 Philosofa

The sofa on the left is the philosophy sofa. A philosopher from a university is sitting on it. Next to him sits the discourse giver. Usually this is a viewer who has left a philosophical contribution or comment on the intranet on the profile of the Phanta Philo Sofa Show that many users have liked. On the Philosofa, people talk about laws, not just paragraphs. These are commandments that regularisation life, like virtues, faith or conscience. So discussions can be broken down into the three areas. Firstly, the factual area; secondly, the area that concerns the identity of a person or group; and thirdly, the area that concerns conscience.

If, for example, people talk about race because an auditor has asked the question: "Are all humans the same?", then firstly the factual level is examined. Scientific findings from biology and ethnology are consulted and the division of humans into species, race and nation is justified. Secondly, the identity of humans is examined, which shows similarities and differences to other humans. Here cultural, religious and family influences are considered. Thirdly, conscience is used to illustrate how every human has a moral compass in his or her head, which is aligned with his or her own principles and those of others.

As soon as a law touches the part of conscience, purely factual arguments no longer work. The people must now jointly consider what the law should be so that the majority of the

---

56Ministry of State Organisation - 8.5.9 Ethics Commission

citizens can reconcile it with their conscience. This negotiation takes place in an ethics committee and is supported by the Phanta Philo Sofa Show. The result will be introduced into the legislative process.

7.2.3.8.2 Phantasofa

The sofa on the right is the fantasy sofa. A minister whose subject area touches on the discourse sits on it. Next to him, the seat is free. Any audience member who has an imagination of what a satisfactory future might look like may sit here. People from the audience can get up and sit there. Users who want to participate interactively in the show via their People's Computer must share their idea on the show's profile page and hope that many will like their idea, or if the studio scout will decide in favour of their idea. Studio Scouts are support staff who sit at their People's Computer and read users' ideas. There are 4 scouts. Once a scout has decided on an idea, he or she takes a seat on the Phantasofa and announces it. Meanwhile, the idea giver must be reachable via his People's Computer to be videoed into the show. Usually there will be a line of people in the show who want to take a seat on the Phantasofa. For this, there is a queue to join. Scouts must also join this queue. To sort good and bad prospects, there are two queues. The moderator ensures a balanced speaking time for both prospects.

7.2.3.8.3 Films

In order to get philosophical stimuli and explanations, one-act films are pre-produced for the upcoming show. The inserts can use puppets, stuffed animals, persons or virtual characters to re-enact the situations. The one-shots are divided into 5 categories.
1 Kids' stuff: Interpersonal problems that are based on the relationship level and call for balancing justice. These can be conflicts between neighbours, colleagues or families. In a play with dolls or stuffed animals, we explore where the problems

come from and how they can be solved in an exemplary way.
2 Psycho? Logical!: Monologues and dialogues from films, soaps, talk shows, press statements and council debates that fit the theme are analysed with deep hermeneutics. The latent meaning is amusingly acted out by actors or in puppet theatre.
3 Moral apostles: A four-member philosophical Residential Community plays out basic philosophical attitudes together in a series. Each flatmate vehemently represents a stance and acts out his or her behaviour accordingly. Through the interaction with the other flatmates, questions constantly arise for which the flatmates justify themselves to each other. The Kantian type lives according to the principle: do everything as if it could become the law. The Kohlbergian type moralises all behaviour, wants to be on the highest moral level himself, categorises the behaviour of others into levels and asks: On which moral level are you? The utilitarian type follows the principle of utility. His motto is: Do what is useful. Useless behaviour or things are repugnant to him, he criticises them and praises what is useful. The liberal type advocates the way of life: Do what is best for you. He is the egoist among the flatmates, for whom white lies and stealing mouths are the order of the day. He advises other housemates to take more care of themselves and to renounce altruism.
4 Operation-Drive-Power: Professionals, consumers and honorary services are visited at their place of work and asked what drives them. The operation drive asks why the operation is carried out. The distribution drive asks why a product is bought. The turnover drive asks why free time and money are sacrificed for an honorary service. Everywhere the deepening questions are asked about what could be improved and how the future of the appeal, the product or the need could develop.
5 The driving of drives: Humans and their drives are explored and re-enacted. In street surveys, passers-by are asked what drives they or humans in general have. The statements are portrayed in scenes by actors on the street and the onlooking passers-by are asked what they think of the drives portrayed.

7.2.3.9 Playroom

In the show "playroom", the moderators and guests play a card or board game in the studio and a player is connected via the intranet. Users can apply to be a player via the show's profile page and are selected by the editorial team. During the game, the moderator asks the guests questions that are appropriate to them. Guests and players can also ask questions. Guests are politicians or persons with socio-political responsibility, such as an employer president.

7.2.3.10 Ground glass

Similar to "Kalkhofe's Mattscheibe"[57] , the concept here is followed with laws and council debates or politicians' election programmes. Voluntary satirists compete on the intranet for the funniest interpretation of a statement made by politicians on TV. Popular contributions make it into the show and the satirist is often invited to comment freely on various statements made by politicians. Satirists comment in a green box and are edited into the politician's video. If a law has already been filmed, comments can also be made against this background.

7.2.3.11 Jammer

In this show, video contributions from political activists are shown and discussed with the authors. The aim is to capture political activists who do not know in which party they can put forward their needs or are anti-constitutional. On this media stage, the motives of the political activists are to be found out. Viewers and guests from the audience are then asked what must have gone wrong, where the people have lost these activists or disregarded their needs. This show is hosted by the Federal Moderator[58] because he has quick admission to all the other ministries. At the end of the broadcast, if there is no satisfactory outcome for the policy activists, the show is conducted and broadcast in the Solution Finder format on a

---

57https://www.tele5.de/kalkofes-welt/mattscheibe/
58Ministry of State Organisation - 4.4.3 Federal Moderators

fixed date on the Beta channel of Government Television.

7.2.3.12 Criminal case unsolved

This show is similar to the broadcast "Aktenzeichen XY ungelöst".[59] Unsolved criminal cases are presented through re-enacted scenes and then witnesses are sought by telephone, internet and intranet. For this purpose, the Ministry of Security regularly provides the show's editorial team with unsolved criminal cases from the recent past. For regional cases, the show is broadcast on Local Television and for national cases on Government Television. Local police stations may contact the local Local Television directly. If a case remains unsolved, it can be rebroadcast in the Government Television show.

In the studio, in addition to the moderator who announces the various cases, there are also senior investigators and trained professionals. Depending on which case is being heard, a psychologist may be helpful to present the mindset of a criminal, or a specialist auditor from the Company Auditing Agency to explain prohibited corporate actions. The trained professional has expertise to explain to the audience and possible witnesses how the crime will behave in daily life towards the possible witness.

For the case of sexual offences, the psyches and lifestyles of sex offenders are depicted by the psychologist in the studio. For the case of white-collar crime, the business practices, such as negotiations and prices or agreements, are depicted and how criminal behaviour is shown or attempted to be built up.

The show can be produced in the studio or in the mobile studio. For example, in the case of white-collar crime, it might make sense to set up the mobile studio on the company premises to search for witnesses among the employees. As with the committees, the TV boxes[60] are used to give anonymous statements. This time, acrylic glass panes made of frosted glass are set up in front of the cameras so that only the shadow can be seen. Between the recording microphone and the mouth is a mechanism to distort the vote.

59https://www.zdf.de/gesellschaft/aktenzeichen-xy-ungeloest
60Ministry of State Organisation - 9.6.3.7.2 TV Box

7.2.3.13 People's Interrogation

The show People's Interrogation is organised when there has been a crime that has caused great public sympathy. As soon as demonstrations for condolences are announced, the Government Television is informed and convenes an editorial team for this show. The show is organised on a mobile basis by sending a People's Motor Vehicle to the demonstration. After the final rally, the discussion format of the show "Solution Finder" is held together with the mourners. The aim there is to find solutions on how such crimes can be prevented in the future. Part of the panel will be responsible ministers and scientists. The ministers are to rate solutions to what extent they can be implemented by their ministry. Scientists are supposed to assess the psyche and socialisation of the victim and offender in order to determine the mental cause of how the crime could have happened. Therefore, the scientists usually consist of psychologists, psychotherapists, psychiatrists, social psychologists, sociologists and social educators. The researchers either have their research focus in similar living or working environments as the offender or have experience with similar personalities as those of the offender and victim.

If the offender or offenders have not been identified at the time of the condolences, the show will be held later in the studio. It is important to know the offender(s) in order to understand their mental and moral development leading up to the crime. It is important to identify problematic circumstances or events in the offender's life in the show so that the people are mindful of similar circumstances or events or prevent them. Accusations and hostility against the offender, who may still be suspected, are forbidden. This is because it is not about the past crime, but about similar future crimes. The criminal does not appear in the people's interrogation. It is rather about how society has produced such a crime and how it can avoid it in the future.

7.2.3.14 Joke

The satirical show Joke is held after the mobile studios have been deployed. The audience creates the show themselves, only the moderator is provided by Government Television. If the audience still feels like doing satire after a committee or a show in a public place, they can stay and shout "joke". Once enough people do that, they can choose elements of the show and play them themselves. This show is made up of many small elements that are set up as a series and come up again and again during the course of the shows when the opportunity arises. Intranet users can pre-produce necessary videos on the show's profile page. The elements are marked in italics.

Remix: Statements by politicians are edited into satirical embassies, or other statements are put into the mouths of the politicians. Volunteers record the statements in advance.

Preview: Volunteers play news presenter. They describe how the news will develop the coming week as if they knew.

Dialectical: Dialects represent different characters. For example, Norbert Nörgele speaks Saxon and is an angry citizen who lists faults. Sepp Schlaumaier is a Bavarian who makes sayings, gives moral speeches, tells proverbs and jokes. Lars Locker is a Hessian and relaxed optimist who always has suggestions for improvement and can find something positive in everything. Volunteers play one of these characters, or invent their own character with a different dialect.

Brainwashing: The moderator is asked by the audience to slip into a certain character, for example manager, tramp, Scientologist, nun or landlord. The aim is to depict stereotypes and compare them, from bizarre to precarious. The audience and spectators can give further stage directions during the moderator's performance, and must line up behind the audience microphone to do so. The role of moderator can also be played by a voluntary audience member.

Couples games: Voluntary couples are selected from the audience and have to perform certain tasks and win. The deciding factor is speed, which is measured with a stopwatch, and quality, which is decided by the audience.

Unequal teams: Unequal teams are formed of volunteers from the audience, for example old versus young, education party versus business party, couples versus single persons, men versus women. The teams compete against each other in creative and funny games, for example advertising a product, designing or creating something, making up sayings about situations, business or product ideas. The audience decides with its laughter. If there is laughter in the audience, a decibel meter measures the volume. Whoever has the loudest and longest laughs during their round wins.

Closing round: In the closing round, local clubs can introduce themselves or an unknown band plays a new song.

8 News Television[61]

The News Television is a news channel that continuously supports citizens with the latest information affecting the whole country. News Television reporters report from places of action and summarise events. Reporting is objective and covers as many topics as possible from all ministries. Reporting is balanced if at least two positions or points of view are presented on a topic that differ, if not only decision-makers but also citizens have their say, if good and bad news are equally distributed in the course of the broadcast, or if there is also a contribution from citizens' television in as many broadcasts as possible.

The News Television Beta channel shows unabridged press conferences and interviews from which the editors have only shown excerpts in the news. The broadcast does not have to be in real time, but it must take place on the same day and remain available in the Media Directory.

Topics with paid images, such as international football matches or award ceremonies, may not be reported on. This reporting, as well as on gambling, is reserved for the private media broadcasters.

The News Television does not show documentaries, feature films or shows. The news programmes run around the clock and repeat several times a day. As soon as new reports appear, older reports are replaced with them. By rating the broadcasts and contributions, viewers can help determine which news

61 §107.1b Powers of the governments

they consider more important than others.

8.1 Programme

The News Television broadcasts news bulletins throughout the day, constantly adding new items depending on where something is happening. There is the regional news, the national news, the continental news and the international news. All the news is divided into the headings of politics, business, culture and crime.

At the bottom of the screen, the Gross Domestic Product[62] of the economic forms, the exchange rates of the domestic currencies, the standard of living index, the tax revenues, the state expenditures, debts and profits are displayed.[63] The display is in each case in the form of numbers of a digital clock and red or green arrows together with the percentage rate of change in a scrolling text.

8.1.1 Policy

In the "Policy" section, the day-to-day work of the politicians is presented. Not all ministries will hold a press conference every day because they have decisions or reform projects to announce. But when a minister announces something, it is shown in extracts and commented on by party members from the various party wings. The content can be statistics, legislative initiatives, criticism, legal loopholes, committees of enquiry, referendums or elections of persons.

8.1.2 Economy

The day-to-day work of the companies is presented in the "Economy" section. The economic development in the four economic forms and the domestic stock exchanges is presented in the economic overview. When companies announce

---

62 Ministry of Finance - 10.6 Determination of the Gross Domestic Product
63 Ministry of Finance - 10.5 Living Standard Index, 10.6 Determination of the Gross Domestic Product, 8 State revenues, 9.7.1 Data

innovations or become involved in court proceedings, this is reported. Care is taken to give equal weight to owners, employees and customers. Contents may also include economic growth, order barometers, bankruptcies and records.

8.1.3 Culture

In the "Culture" section, the cultural events of the day are presented. When citizens, clubs or associations celebrate a significant occasion, or engage in controversy because cultural differences have clashed, this is reported. Care is taken to ensure that uninvolved citizens such as neighbours or people of other faiths also have their say. Contents can be events, performances, news of deaths, discoveries and insights. The culture section also provides for hilarity and uses mainly popular contributions from civic television for this purpose.

8.1.4 Crime

All current wanted persons are reported in the "Crime" section. Police wanted persons are reported in the regional or national news, depending on the offence, in the form of a video clip with the course of events, the scene of the crime and the offender's profile. The Ministry of Security reports to the Ministry of Media Affairs all cases that either need a great deal of publicity to track down the offender or cases that have caused great damage to society. Each individual police station sends its unclassified incident reports, via the intranet to the News Television. Here the reports are reviewed and if the editorial meeting votes in favour of reporting, a filming date is arranged with the local police station and a news report is produced.

If cases have been solved through witness statements that came about after the APB in the News Television, this will be mentioned in the section. Images from police officers' body cameras can be used for the "Crime" section. This footage is anonymised before broadcast.

8.1.5 News overview

A Federal Moderator presents the news once a day at 8 p.m. in 15Minuten. In it, positive and negative events that have happened in the country are presented. In one segment, the individual ministers have their say, rating the situations and saying whether they have discovered potential for reform as a result of an event.

On Sundays, the newsreel runs for 45 minutes, in which all the events from the news are each wrapped up in a history of how they developed over the course of the week.

The monthly show runs for 90 minutes on the last Sunday of the month and is produced in exactly the same way as the newsreel. Events are followed for weeks and months as long as they were shown in the daily news.

The annual review lasts 120 minutes and is produced twice. Once before the budget vote, where only the financial expenditure and the work done by the 18 ministries is presented. In the second annual review, the events of the news year are summarised at the end of the calendar year.

8.1.5.1 Archive system

The News Television creates an archive system in the Media Directory via its news reviews. There, citizens can use their People's Computer to quickly and easily find information from previous years to make their voting decision in an informed state for a budget vote, an election of persons or a legislative vote.

As a review of the year, the course of the year is listed in a timeline. The timeline is constructed in dots and dashes. Sometimes there are dots that represent an event of a day, for example when a new solar cell was invented. Sometimes there are dashes that represent a progression over days or weeks. Depending on how strong the effects were, the lines are thicker or thinner. Depending on the duration, they are longer or shorter, for example in the case of a flood and clean-up work. Sometimes there are broken lines and dots, such as a plane crash with recovery work, flight data recorder evaluation, court proceedings, verdict and victim compensation. The representation looks like this (._. ___ . _).

Depending on which colour is used, the respective ministry has been involved or a multi-coloured design of the lines and strokes if several ministries have been involved.

8.1.6 At the table at the party congress

When party congresses are held, the News Television comes to the party congress site with its mobile dining room studio and interviews the top representatives of all party wings and the minister or ministers about their views on the proposals for the party programme. For as long as the party congress lasts, the top representatives and ministers meet for breakfast, lunch and dinner in the dining room studio.

The studio is an ISO container whose side walls are glazed. In the centre is a large oval table with chairs. Two oval concentric rails run along the ceiling, one large outside, one small inside. In each of these rails are two swivelling cameras on trolleys so that all the participants can be filmed. There is a 360° camera in the table and directional microphones are hidden in the flower vases on the table. In the middle of the table there is a computer that can be opened and put down to watch video contributions from the party wings. These video contributions are shown large in the broadcast image when the moderator refers to them during questions.

Food is provided by local restaurants, which are superimposed at the bottom of the screen as long as their services are visible. A keg of beer is served with dinner. After the hour at dinner, the remaining beer is poured out to party participants, who are allowed to drink it together. The dining table in the studio now becomes the regulars' table. As soon as the beer glass is empty and you want to get another one, you have to move away from the table and make room for the next volunteer who has never sat at the table before. The transmission continues in the Beta channel and lasts until the beer keg is empty, but for a maximum of 2 hours. Statements from the dinner table or regulars' table are source material for news programme contributions.

9 Local Television

The Local Television consists of many regional stations. It is responsible for municipal policy in the respective catchment area. The Local Television's broadcasts are only broadcast within the affected areas, but are available throughout the country via the Media Directory.

Particular emphasis is placed on areas that have transferred responsibilities from the national level to the municipal level by subsidiarity vote. The aim is to make the policies of municipalities, cultural protection areas and economic zones accessible to the media. The broadcasting centres are located in the capital cities, in the same broadcasting centre as Government Television. When features are produced, camera crews travel to the location. All municipal policy events are covered by Government Television staff unless citizens volunteer to do so and also provide balanced and objective reports. Citizens can lend out material from the broadcast centre to make their own film productions.

9.1 Regional Citizen Television

Each municipality gets a regional channel on the intranet where the citizens produce television together. The channel is available via the Media Directory and each regional channel is given a profile. Groups can be formed in the profile to form an editorial team. Each group occupies a rubric. The rubrics are determined by each new editorial team itself by joining an existing rubric or founding a new rubric and setting up there. So-called editorial groups gather voluntary reporters, editors, cameramen and media designers. Voluntary cameramen upload their video footage to the Local Television server so that all group members can access and edit it together. After editing, the result is finished video clips, documentaries, feature films or shows. Users can be members of as many newsrooms as they like, so groups can help each other out with footage and staff. For investigative research teams, several groups can join together, consisting of voluntary reporters for news.

Citizen television is produced through co-productions with the Local Television or independently by the citizens and broadcast to the Local Television. All contributions are uploaded to the Media Directory and rated by users. Popular contributions are broadcast in the Local Television programme. If audience ratings are high, the video footage is sent to the Party Television's Nationwide Citizen Television.

9.2 Programme

The programme consists of the daily news of a region, documentaries, feature films and shows. Feature films are only produced by the citizens themselves. All other contributions are produced by the citizens either on their own or in co-production with Local Television. An algorithm takes over the programming, when which contribution is shown, based on the target group, time and length of the contribution. The automatically generated programme schedule is available for voting on the profile page. Users can change the programme line-up through their majority ratings.

9.2.1 News

There is news on Local Television every day. The news programme lasts 15 minutes, unless a municipal policy decision is to be made interactively. In the case of a municipal committee or other direct-democratic decision-making by the municipality, a special news broadcast is made. The scheduled broadcasts are shown on the Beta channel.

9.2.1.1 Voluntary reporters

All citizens can become free news reporters. To do so, they make videos either with their smartphone, camera or People's Computer. Persons who can be recognised on the video must agree to the recordings or be made unrecognisable. Videos made with the People's Computer can be shared directly in the Media Directory. Videos shot with a smartphone or camera are uploaded to the internet via the Local Television website. This requires an account registered to a citizen. The videos are sent by the Ministry of Media Affairs to the Ministry of Digital Affairs and from there uploaded on the intranet to the servers of the Media Directory. Either the videos are first shared and edited only with an editorial group of Regional Citizen Television or all users can comment and rate the contributions directly on the profile page of the Local Television in the Media Directory.

Editors of the state television select contributions that fit their broadcasts. Features that have high viewership in the Media Directory are broadcast in the Local Television and forwarded to the Nationwide Citizen Television.

The news from the citizens is divided into categories, for example good or bad news. The length of the videos is decided by the citizens. Ready-cut contributions with a length of up to 2 minutes are included in the regional news programme of the day, "Citizen News". This broadcast is divided into the categories of politics, work, leisure and family. Everywhere there is a distinction between good and bad news. The order in which the bad and good news is broadcast is decided by the citizens in the editorial group. The news editorial group makes its decisions publicly and democratically on the profile of the news programme in the Media Directory.

9.2.1.2 Interview Ralley

All citizens can become rally reporters. All they have to do is register on a list at their local Local Television via the Media Directory. Reporter Ralleys are conducted on hot topics. Ralley reporters can be used by all state broadcasters for news programmes, shows or other formats for investigation. As soon as it has been decided in an editorial meeting, all registered Ralley Reporters receive a message on their People's Computer. The message will state the broadcaster, format, starting time, target group and subject area. Those who register for the rally will receive the questions on their People's Computer at the start time.

The rally is organised in such a way that teams of 2 get together.

One operates the camera and the other interviews people. The teams change every hour. Depending on which target group a survey covers, the rally reporters have to interview passers-by, work colleagues, friends or family. It is about a central question posed by the editorial team. Sometimes it can also be a questionnaire.

The first round of the rally is won by the first person to upload all the questions answered by all the persons. The number of people, as well as the questions, will be determined by the editors.

The winner of the second round of the rally will be the first person to compile a 30-second contribution, including background text, from all the answers.

The third and final round is won by whoever has the most viewers and good ratings after one week.

The overall rally is won by whoever could achieve the best placements among all participants in the overall average in all three rounds. The winner receives prize money equivalent to the usual wage for a finished news report.

9.2.2 Documentaries

Residents of a city can make any documentary on any topic. Only a series is specified into which the documentary is to fit.

9.2.2.1 City talk

This documentary is produced as an ongoing series. Each city is an episode, each theme is a season. The inaugural season has as its theme the milieu in different neighbourhoods. Questions to the inhabitants of different neighbourhoods could be: What do people in one neighbourhood think about the other neighbourhoods? Where would they like to live, where not and why? What do they think about life, love and work? Citizens conduct interviews with each other at places they have chosen in the city where they live.

9.2.3 Feature films

Feature films can be produced by citizens on their own initiative. How long the feature films last is left up to the directors. Through the digital networking of editorial groups, feature films can be produced in different locations by local editorial groups, with only the main actors travelling around the country for the production. Nationwide Citizen Television is responsible for feature films nationwide.

9.2.4 Shows

The shows on the democratic management of elections of persons and legislation are implemented for the municipal administered ministries with the same shows as in the Government Television. The usual regions can develop their own shows or use the following show formats.

9.2.4.1 City presentation

Each city makes documentary videos and a show together with Local Television. In the documentary videos, municipal institutions such as the waste disposal centre, sewage treatment plant, town hall, fire brigade or school are presented. In the show, these videos are shown first and then the employees are talked to about them. Workers are asked if something strange, dangerous or funny happened, or how the work could be done faster, better, cheaper or funnier. Together with the audience, successful strategies are to be found and shared. After the employees have had their turn, the audience guests, all city residents, are now allowed to express praise, criticism and suggestions for improvement.

9.2.4.2 Hard drinking and true to the line

Two regulars' tables with different party-political orientations compete against each other. So if you meet frequently in a pub and usually talk about politics, you can sign up for the show with your fellow regulars at the local Television.

Registration is done via a regular's computer on the show's profile page in the Media Directory. The registration form lists all participants, the location and the policy. In addition, it should be ticked off which subject areas of the 18 ministries are being talked about, which buzzwords apply and which party wings the participants' statements are close to.

Now the editorial team can find two teams that have a similar or an opposite orientation. This database is nationwide. The show is organised similar to a tournament. First, local regulars compete against each other. The profits then compete in North, South, East or West competitions, which are broadcast on Local Television by several regional stations involved. At the end, the winner is determined in a nationwide show broadcast on Nationwide Citizen Television.

The rules of the competition are similar to the rules of "Truth or Dare". A topic is put in the room by the moderator and both regulars' tables discuss it separately. After 5 to 10 minutes, a bottle is turned on each regulars' table. The person to whom the bottle points is allowed to decide for truth or duty. If one decides for "truth", one has to name the culprit(s) of a problem and why one is angry about the problem. If one chooses "duty", one must present a solution to the problem and name the responsible authorities.

Afterwards, the audience and spectators vote by People's Computer whether they agree or disagree with the speaker and whether they liked the presentation style or not.

In the next round, the moderator presents a new problem and the procedure begins again. In each round, the participants are given new drinks. At the end of all the rounds, all the votes from viewers and the audience from all the rounds are added up. The table that received the most votes wins the game in this broadcast and qualifies for the regional or national championships.

10 Party Television[64]

The Party Television is the broadcaster for the parties and ministries. With the staff of the Party Television, the workers of the ministries and the working groups of the party wings develop the content with which they present their work. The work presented is intended to inform state management. Where a ministry is administered municipally, it also has the right to use the Party Television if the Ministry of Media Affairs is not administered municipally. If a ministry has been communitarised by an International Union, the programme will be extended to the participants in the thematic area of the affected ministry.

Party Television is responsible for informing citizens about all state activities. Content is produced in co-production with all ministries. All visits are announced and discussed with each other in advance. The format in which the content is to be implemented is also decided here. The Ministry of Media Affairs and the responsible ministry present their results as a documentary, feature film or show. For example, a broadcast comes from the school and its lessons or the daily work of the authorities such as the Tax Office or the police. Together with the film team, the employees create the story that is written about the typical working day. The viewer should be able to feel part of this story. The contact between state employee and citizen must be found in every film. In feature films, the employees are the actors, although not necessarily in their traditional positions. Documentaries are presented in the form of a biography. A focal person is singled out by the Party Television filmmakers, their workplace is documented and all colleagues are introduced.

Party Television has broadcasting centres in the capital cities of the ministries. The headquarters is in the capital city of the Ministry of Media Affairs, while the other broadcasting centres take care of proximity to the local film and television studios. For filming outside the broadcasting centres, a separate vehicle fleet is set up with campers, buses and transport trucks. This fleet can be used either to send an entire film crew across the country or to take individual film teams on week-long

---

64§71.3 Review of effectiveness, §107.1b Powers of governments

expeditions to the offices and authorities.

10.1 Programme[65]

In the programme of the Party Television is the nationwide continuous filming of all activities of all ministries, the constitution and party programmes. Activities change as soon as laws change. The constitution changes as soon as articles are added, reworded or deleted. The daytime programme consists mainly of series and documentaries; shows and feature films are shown in the evenings and at night. Newly established companies and associations in Planned Economy and Social Market Economy can advertise as an advertising break between features. During the election week, there is a focus coverage on the relevant topic. There is no news on Party Television.

10.1.1 Documentaries

The documentary films document the work in the individual ministries. All ministries are shown at the same time, so that some ministries are not documented continuously and others not at all for months.

10.1.1.1 Ministries internal

This documentary is produced as a series. Each ministry has a season and each area, such as departments, authorities and field offices are depicted in one episode each. It is crucial that all areas and especially all cost centres listed in the budget vote are depicted.
Editors prepare the screenplays, stroyboards and shooting schedules in cooperation with the responsible ministry staff. Interviews are conducted with the responsible staff and the clients on how the services are provided. All work processes are filmed.

---

65 §113,3b,5 Media democracy

10.1.1.2 Milieu meetings

The Ministry of Integration discloses its clustering and illustrates it through this documentary. Clustering means dividing the population into different strata, milieus and interest groups. It is the task of the Ministry of Integration to reconcile the milieus with each other through education and, if necessary, demarcation.

This documentary is set up as a series and is supplemented with a show. In one episode, about 3 different life stories of different characters are shown. These are the focus characters. All characters belong to the same milieu, for example subcultures, religions, professional groups, celebrities or residential areas. In the course of a season, more and more relationships are established between the characters. These can be supply chains, subculture meetings, churches or pavements. At the end of a season, the focal persons get to know each other in the show. In the show, the focus persons from the same milieu are informed about their milieu with scientific research results. They can describe their experiences and whether these correspond to the research results. Viewers can use their People's Computer via the intranet to comment and rate what makes this milieu special and what problems it might cause for other humans. In this show, the Minister of Integration also sits on the panel next to the focus persons and scientists.

After one season, the milieu is changed. The characters are newly selected by the editorial team. For this purpose, the Ministry of Media Affairs accesses the data records of the intranet to calculate who from which milieu might meet. During the recordings, the focus persons continue to go about their daily lives and are accompanied by a camera team for a week.

10.1.1.3 Transparent state service

This documentary is co-produced with the Ministry of State Organisation. The aim is to explain all political structures, such as ministries, parties and councils with their meaning, as well as the processes of elections of persons, governments, committees, voting and quorums.[66] For this purpose, vehicles are equipped with action cameras and persons with body cameras, so that the flow of information can be depicted. The channels of state and citizen entities are represented here in the first-person perspective (POV Point of View). The wearers of the cameras or drivers of the vehicles can speak in background text if they wish. Party Television staff edit the documentary according to the storyboard, which has been voted with the State Organisation Minister. All footage is posted on the intranet and can be rated by users. If a practice seen displeases users, i.e. domestic nationals, they can mention this in a comment and additionally report the comment to the Surveillance Television. The possible grievance will then be investigated by Surveillance Television.

10.1.1.4 Weekend

This documentary is produced as a series. In each episode, the minister and voluntary employees of the ministry are accompanied by cameras for a weekend. Whether the footage is shot with a camera crew or privately with cameras handed out is decided by the actors themselves; after all, it is their privacy they are giving insight into. Each season, a different ministry takes its turn.

The schedule of a usual weekend is discussed by the actor and the director. Limits of privacy are set, which the camera team is not allowed to exceed during the filming. Before the broadcast, the protagonist must agree to the finished edited video material and can request changes if necessary.

10.1.1.5 Medical television

All treatments listed in the Health Directory are filmed, recorded and edited by a camera team. Care must be taken to ensure that the persons giving treatment also announce

---

66Ministry of State Organisation - 8 Political structure, 9 Political processes

each work step they do, if possible. This work is done when all available treatments in the Health Directory have been videoed. From then on, only new treatments are filmed once. Accordingly, the filming schedule is based on the medical fee schedule.[67] These videos are checked by the students of health care in a written examination and thus also by a chair of the university hospitals. At the end, the Ministry of Education sends the correction results to the Ministry of Media Affairs and, if there are no treatment errors, they are published in the Health Directory, Knowledge Directory and Party Television. The Ministry of Health cooperates with the Party Television film team.

In addition to this video, every treated patient can produce his own video for his own treatment with his People's Computer. For this purpose, there is a special programme that tells you what you should film and in which picture setting so that the video is appealing and comprehensible. These patient reports can be accessed via the Health Directory and are analysed by Party Television in cooperation with the colleges. Matching videos about the recovery processes are put together with the matching diseases and treatment methods in the documentary film about the treatment of a diagnosis.

10.1.2 Feature films

The Party Television produces feature films depicting the constitution, party programmes or the work of the ministries.

10.1.2.1 Constitution filming

The constitution is filmed as a series to make it easier to insert constitutional amendments. Each article is an episode and each chapter is a season. After a constitutional committee and before voting on it, Party Television must have produced the episode so that voters can better understand the article and its implications.

---

67 Ministry of Health - 5.5 Medical Fee Schedule

10.1.2.2 Party programme filming

This feature film will be produced as a series. The screenplay will be based on the party programme. Each programme item is an episode, each chapter a season. The parties work together with an experienced scriptwriter from Party Television to develop a story that represents the programme. From this, a screenplay is created in which the story and the appearance of the characters are given. Voluntary film teams are formed from party members of the respective working groups and voluntary citizens. Voluntary film teams look for suitable actors of the respective age of the main character from birth to death. Each film team decides on a 5-year period in the life of the main character. The main characters should look similar enough to each other at a different age. If there are many voluntary film teams, the time span is shortened. In this way, a long series can be created in a short time, in which the film teams divide up the episodes and seasons. In the Media Directory, users can work interactively on the storyboard for the screenplay and coordinate rooms, actors or staff on location. The editing can then be carried out by several editorial groups and virtually in the editing programme of the Media Directory.

The film teams take care of the filming in the real world and upload the files to the server of the Ministry of Media Affairs. Other users can access this and cut everything at the same time according to the screenplay, by each participant in the film editing selecting a time slot that is then blocked for others. Until the whole film has been cut once, a time slot cannot be cut twice. Users in the Media Directory can look at the rough cuts and rate them interactively, find majorities and perhaps convince the filmmakers to cut or even shoot another version, as long as the story in the screenplay is not changed.

Production does not necessarily have to be done by voluntary film crews, but can also be produced by Party Television. Election programmes are produced by the Government Television in feature films, which may or may not be based on the story from the party programme series.

10.1.2.3 Genres for different ministries

All feature films are to be based on true events. Party Television scriptwriters are given access to the archives of the ministries to facilitate screenplay writing. As a principle, the films should have a good ending, because the aim of politics is to improve the lives of humans, not to make them worse. The editors of Party Television propose to divide the ministries into appropriate genres.

State organisation is depicted in the genre of science fiction when political structures and processes have changed. Domestic politics is depicted as an action film with, for example, terrorism, civil war and racial riots. Foreign policy is portrayed as a war film from the declaration of war to the conduct of war, peace negotiations and diplomatic relations between the once hostile states. Labour politics is staged as a comedy with relationships of wealth and poverty and relationships with colleagues. Family policy is portrayed in a love story from marriage to divorce to funeral. Education policy is filmed as a drama between research urges and ethical dubiousness. Economic policy is portrayed as an agent thriller with lobbying, stock market speculation, bankruptcies and hostile takeovers. Fiscal policy uses a doomsday film to demonstrate national bankruptcy and how the economy can be restarted. Security policy occupies the genre of crime film, in which crimes and their solving are depicted. The feature films of justice policy do not have a happy ending, with criminals committing serious crimes such as murder and manslaughter, as in a horror film, but ultimately receiving their just sentence.

10.1.2.4 Film Festival

Every year, the best feature films produced in whole or in part by state television are selected. There are categories for films of different lengths, for different genres as well as for films produced by citizens, the state or both together. In all categories there are sections for the best films, directors, cinematographers, media designers, leading actors and supporting actors. There is prize money for each category.

The users of the Media Directory make a pre-selection by nominating all films seen on state television in the archive or directly after the video for the film competition. If enough users can be found, the film will be screened at the film festival. The festival lasts one week and takes place in all participating cinemas. At the end of each film, all cinema-goers are asked to give their opinion. All categories are asked for on a scale of 1 to 6. At the end of the week, the media minister counts the votes and awards the prizes.

10.1.3 Shows

The shows on Party Television deal with the content of the ministries, with the politicians as humans and with the citizens as voluntary interactive helpers in the service of the ministries.

10.1.3.1 A little fun is a must

The show "A little fun is a must" is produced together with the ministries of economy. The show takes place at the premises of participating companies. According to the Right to Fun at Work[68] , surveys are sent out to companies, which office wants to present its measures for more fun at work in the show. For example, office toys and cameras will be installed in an open-plan office. After a week, the best scenes are edited together and shown in the show.

The boss and the appearing employees are invited to the show. The jokers are allowed to say what would have to happen for them to have fun, or why they were not in a fun mood at the time recorded. Staff members at whose expense fun was being had may voice this on the show. If bullying is identified, excusions must be written and expressed on the show. If necessary, the rules of the show will be adjusted.

At the end of the show, the viewers and the guests vote on which measure for more fun they found the funniest. The show's editors maintain a database in which all the measures are stored. Users can view and rate them via the show's profile

---

68 Ministry of Labour - 16.5 Fun at work

page in the Media Directory. Companies can get suggestions from this about what they would like to offer.

10.1.3.2 A little bit of hate must be

The show "A little bit of hate must be" is produced together with the Ministry of Family Affairs. The show informs about hate and shares what is hated. There are three sections for this, which alternate. The show aims to take hate out of the taboo zone so that it can be analysed and avoided. The show explains and shows how hate comes about.

The moderator leafs through a "What is what" book that has been reissued by the editors and is now called "What is hate". He recites the form of hate that is in the foreground on the day of the broadcast and explains its scientific mode of action in the fear-hate circuit.

Bet hate...?" specifically provokes the kind of hate, with envy, jealousy, injustice, rudeness, anger and fright, that is the focus of the show's respective broadcast. Using hidden cameras, hate situations are provoked with passers-by. Before the escalation, the guests in the studio can bet on what kind of hater the victim is. The fear-hate circuit is explained. Active haters use violence against things or other humans. Passive haters use hate against themselves.

On the show's profile, a So-called "hate book" is put online as an anti-social terror network, which is supposed to form an antipole to Facebook or the Persons Directory, which are social networks. Here, users can create profiles that they hate and use their admission to the Persons Directory to get rid of their hate. Viewers may and should give free rein to their hatred, devalue and comment. Threats of criminal offences are prohibited. Only swear words and reasons for hating someone are permitted.

You can "add someone as an enemy", which is the same as the friend request. With the "hate button" you can express your hatred about the actions of your enemies. It replaces the "Like" button. Enemy pages can be created. These are similar to fan pages of public persons or institutions. One can despise these enemy images, which otherwise corresponds to following them. The hate book is a preventive measure to be able to express hatred so that it does not escalate into psychological violence. Enemies can clearly express their opinions here, and do so as coarsely as would otherwise be forbidden. Threats remain punishable, because hate is not allowed to leave the hate book. What is in the hate book remains in the hate book. All participants from "Bet hate...?" and the "Hate book" are invited to the show and advised and reconciled by an expert team of psychologists, pedagogues and sociologists.

10.1.3.3 Think Tank

The Think Tank show is a production for the Ministry of Innovation and in particular for the People's Innovation Company Think Tank[69] . Voluntary groups of inventors from the Ideas Directory can find other inventors through the Think Tank show to work together on an invention or innovation. This can be goods, services and work steps. For example, a Think Tank for a flying car might be looking for a Think Tank to work on marketing and sales, or an environmentally neutral way of production. In a broadcast, a Think Tank working alone is presented, supported and networked, or Think Tanks working together are presented and supported. The presentation is done on the one hand by camera teams visiting the inventor groups, filming first results and the way of working, and on the other hand by inviting the inventor group to the studio. Support is provided by inviting expert scientists and Company Auditing Agency staff to the panel, to whom the inventor group can ask any questions.

The editorial team strives to have Think Tanks that are as diverse as possible, from different members, such as old, young, male or female, or from the different remits of the 18 ministries. The aim is to cover a comprehensive range of topics in order to be able to report in a versatile way.

If viewers want to join the Inventors' Group, support it beyond the broadcast or collaborate with it commercially, they can find the link to the Ideas Directory profile via the show's profile page to get in touch.

69 Ministry of Innovation - 11 People's Innovation Company Think Tank

10.1.3.4 Crowdfunding

The show "Crowdfunding" is produced together with the Ministry of Innovation. Anyone who wants to launch a novelty and has a profile in the Ideas Directory registered on the crowdfunding platform[70] can apply for the crowdfunding show. Those who apply will have their presentation video displayed on the show's profile page in the Media Directory and can be rated by viewers. The most popular applicants will be invited to the show.

New companies can solicit employees and start-up capital. Depending on what is being sought on the crowdfunding platform, potential employees or investors are invited to the show. Investors can become shareholders and buy a share in the company. Or they can be savers who buy shares or bonds in the company through the People's Stock Exchange. Or it can be users of the crowdfunding platform who donate amounts of money and receive a thank-you gift in kind from the company in return.

Similar to the show "Die Höhle der Löwen"[71], the ideas are presented. Funding, recruitment and implementation are clarified with the responsible bodies in the show. Investors hold a casting for inventors or entrepreneurs with the best business idea. Entrepreneurs hold a casting for the best employees.

The show is recorded and lasts a whole day because several companies present themselves and only the best parts are cut together in the show. This way, the entrepreneurs can decide what to cut out to avoid piracy. But the show can also be produced and broadcast in real time and then resembles a fundraising gala where viewers can send money in real time via the crowdfunding platform.

This show is additionally produced on a mobile basis at trade fairs. All innovations from the Ideas Directory that are represented at a domestic fair are invited to the mobile studio on the fairground.

---

70 Ministry of Innovation - 8.3 Crowdfunding Platform
71 https://www.vox.de/cms/sendungen/die-hoehle-der-loewen.html

10.1.3.5 Job market

The ministries of labour and economy fulfil two tasks through the show. Firstly, they show how labour is placed in the different types of companies, industries and economic forms. Secondly, vacancies and job applicants become visible, allowing other companies to recruit vacancies or persons to train or upskill for vacancies. Companies and applicants taking part in the show are either contacted by the editors because they fit the theme of the broadcast, or they independently fill out the application form on the show's profile page in the Media Directory. Those who want to take part in the show have to upload a video application. Companies present the jobs, applicants present themselves and their CVs. At least one work step is set up on the stage in the studio, which has to be performed in the course of the job. The applicants perform the work steps and ask questions or make suggestions for improvement. Their skills are observed by possible colleagues who usually perform this activity and are assessed afterwards. At the end of the show, the recruiters ask all the applicants they have selected whether they want the job or not.

10.1.3.6 Mini-Minister

This show follows ministers who are new in office and have to complete various internships in their ministry.[72] The viewers can choose in which area the minister is to work. The ministry staff tell him what activities he does there. In short interviews, the minister is asked how he feels and how he finds the work. Workers are asked how they rate the work the minister has done for them.

10.1.3.7 Remorse

The show consists of excerpts from video contributions by politicians or decision-makers. Self-talks of different roles are staged. The conscience of politicians and decision-makers is staged. At a certain point, the video clip is stopped and

72Ministry of State Organisation - 9.9.4.11 Familiarisation

one character becomes three identical clones. Figuratively, two identical-looking persons step out of the original person. During the time the original person is not talking, their imagined thoughts are spoken by the two clones. The two clones are like angels and devils on shoulders or like the psychic superego and id. If the politicians or decision-makers want to, they are allowed to say in a video to the editor what they were really thinking at that time.

10.1.3.8 Tops of the week

The tops of the week show the most popular media content of the past week. Popularity is determined by the ratings and views of the media content. The media content comes from state media, companies or private individuals. The videos that have achieved the highest ratings and most clicks in the past week are shown. The videos are automatically collected from all directories of the intranet.
Content includes, for example, videos from the crowdfunding platform[73] , training videos on strength, endurance and stretching from the Club Directory and Knowledge Directory, songs with the most views on all music sites on the internet and intranet. From the internet, trailers of movies with the most views and downloads are shown, as well as funny videos from video platforms. Citizen TV provides homemade songs with music video, dubbing of a video and videos of recreational sports.

10.1.3.9 Language students

This show looks for words that were introduced to trivialise other words. The meanings behind the words at the time are shown. Matching archive footage will be sought. The aim of the show is to show how language was changed in order to deceive citizens or to place the terms in the context of a new insight or a new attitude to life.
On the show's intranet page, citizens can enter words they

---

73 Ministry of Innovation - 8.3 Crowdfunding Platform

think are soft and what the same thing used to be called. In order not to leave the selection entirely up to the editors, users can vote on the citizens' proposals. The most popular words are then investigated.

The word and the unword of the year will be chosen in special broadcasts. Voting will again take place in advance via the show's profile page in the Media Directory.

10.1.3.10 Advertising review

In this show, promotional videos are critically scrutinised, subjected to scientific tests and satirically restaged. These promotional videos can come from parties or companies and should be familiar from the media. However, if a foreign company also sells inland, an advertising video from foreign television can also be used.

For example, the commercial videos are reversed or the setting in which the action takes place is completely changed. For example, in a commercial for water, the water could be drunk by an athlete who has just done sport. In the new advertising video, the water could be drunk by someone who has just vomited, drinks the water and vomits again immediately. To report on the water sales of a corporation inland and in comparison in a water-scarce area of the world, the new commercial can also show thirsty humans without money who cannot afford the water that comes from a source in their area. They perform the same action as in the commercial, only without water. In the case of parties, new proposals or programmes could produce the opposite effect under unfavourable circumstances. Here the action remains the same, but under different circumstances.

10.1.3.11 Television makes theatre

In this show, guests invited by the wheel action perform improvisational theatre together with voluntary guests from the audience. The party wings are responsible for the sets and roles, the actors for the role distribution and behaviour.

The tickets for this show are expensive so that the audience guests are motivated to take part and want to be on TV. The actors are amateurs from the audience and guests invited by the editors.

10.1.3.11.1 Party work

The sets and roles come from party members of different party wings and are about currently discussed issues in their party. Ideally, they are party members from the party wing that provides the minister and party members from opposition party wings. They design situations in the appropriate working groups on how a policy can succeed or fail. Party wings are free to depict the failure of another party wing's policy or to portray their own policy as successful.

All parties are given access to a computer programme to create the stage sets. It enables the virtual construction of a stage and offers a fundus of scenery, furniture, objects and costumes that can be distributed on the semicircular stage. The available furniture and objects are the things that are in fact also available in the show's fundus. Roles are defined for each stage set, but not their behaviour. The set and costume designers are able to make new items for the stage or tailor new costumes.

Party members who have created the sets and thought up the roles are invited to the show and take their seats in the front row of the audience.

10.1.3.11.2 Guests

The guests include at least one actor, other guests are politicians, celebrities, scientists, business leaders or representatives of large associations. The editors select the guests to match the sets and roles. The party wings can fill out a wish list of guests for the editors.

The guests are already told all the sets and roles of the broadcast in their invitation and can accept or not accept the invitation accordingly. During a play, not all guests play at the same time, but perform one after the other. Meanwhile, guests who are not acting or rehearsing wait with the moderator on the sofa. There they can discuss whether they want to perform together or only with people from the audience. The guests on the sofa can see all the stage sets of the broadcast and the corresponding roles. On the sofa is a tablet PC with photos of all the digitally created stage sets and descriptions of all the roles. The guests decide together who would like to take part in which set and which role they would like to have. As soon as the desired stage set is turned into the studio, the guest stands in the circle next to it. If necessary, several guests can also go into the circle. Whether they get their desired role depends on the majority decision of each acting group.

10.1.3.11.3 Roles

For each stage set, the party wings propose roles to be filled. How many role proposals there are is up to the party members. Whether all the roles can be filled is decided as soon as it is clear how many volunteers there are in an acting group. Each acting group will distribute the roles independently and think up their own actions. In the dressing room, make-up and rehearsal room, the actors talk aloud about their roles and exchange ideas. If they need help with staging, there is an acting teacher and director backstage. Who does what, however, is ultimately decided by the acting group itself and must do so at the latest as soon as the discussed action is over and the improvisation part begins.

10.1.3.11.4 Studio setup

The studio consists of two revolving stages and a grandstand where guests and moderator sit on a central sofa, behind which the grandstand for the audience rises.
To the right and left of the sofa for the moderator and guests, there are two circles in which volunteers from the audience and one or more guests stand to form an acting team. New teams are formed on an ongoing basis so that there is a continuous

play on two revolving stages.

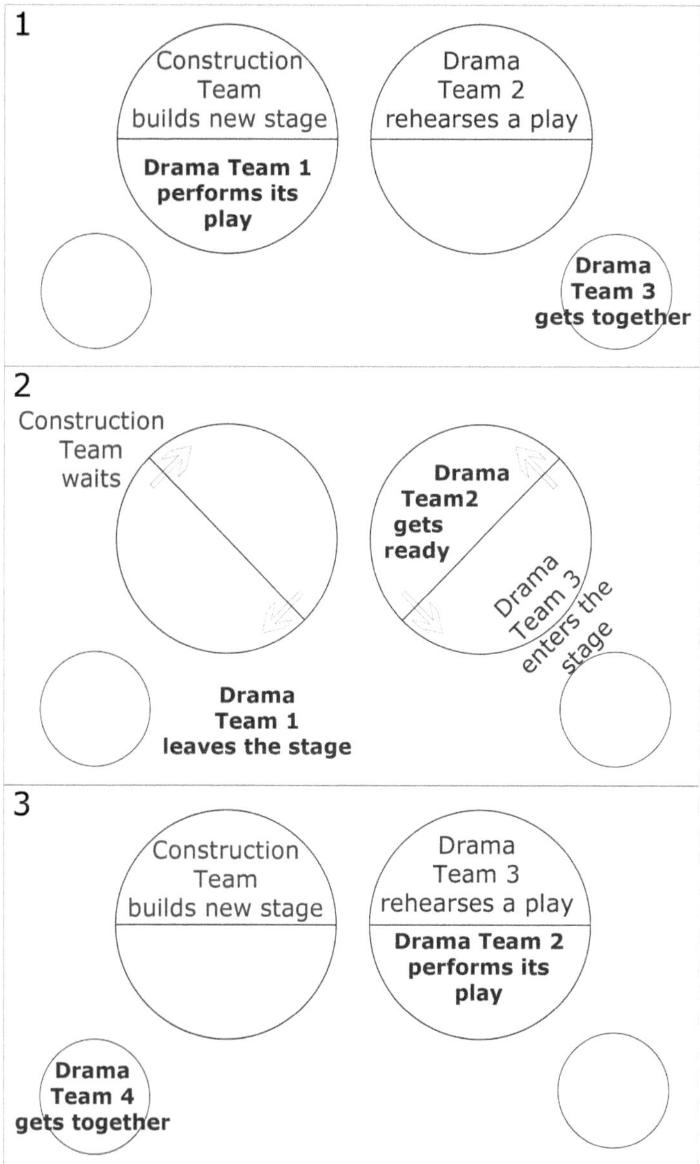

While the play is being performed on one revolving stage at the front, the stage set is being rebuilt behind it. On the other revolving stage, the set of the next play but one is visible at the front for the guests and the audience. On the wall next to each circle is a display board showing the roles to be cast. Whoever wants to play there has to stand in the circle. As soon as a play is finished, both stages turn. First, the team leaves the stage on the left where they have just played. At the same time, the team leaves the circle and moves to the right stage. Now both stages turn. The newly built stage set appears on the left and the next team on the right. As soon as the team went out of the circle onto the stage, it is rotated. Each revolving stage has a door in the middle wall, i.e. the back wall of the stages, so that there is more freedom in whether to use doors to let actors walk up and down from the stage. Backstage, there is a strict whispering tone during set construction and rehearsals. Outside the studio there is a rehearsal room, make-up and dressing rooms. A team's rehearsals are held in the soundproof rehearsal room backstage.

10.1.3.11.5 Procedure

The moderator comes in and presents the two sets on the revolving stages and the guests for today's show. The first two plays are developed by the guests together before the show. They are performed without an audience, but with all the guests and the moderator together.

The performances on the two revolving stages run alternately one after the other. The audience sees a set for the first time when it is turned into the studio. The roles to be cast appear simultaneously on the scoreboard. From then on, all volunteers can stand in the circle until there are enough persons in the circle to fill all the roles.

New acting groups are formed all the time. A complete team consists of a minimum of 5 and a maximum of 10 people. The team leaves the circle as soon as it is complete and goes on stage, which was not currently being played, as soon as the current play is finished. Backstage, they think up their play up to a certain point in the plot and improvise the rest.

Each play is interrupted after 10 minutes. However, the audience and the spectators can decide by quorum whether it should be extended by 10 minutes. For this purpose, the audience guests have remote controls and the audience members have their People's Computers. In the middle between the two revolving stages, hangs a digital clock that counts down from 10 minutes. After each play, each participating party wing is given 30 seconds to speak. In it, the party members explain why they have chosen the stage set and the roles. If possible, they can also act out their justifications on the stage they have created.

When the broadcasting time is almost over, no new team is allowed to line up. The team with the last performance then plays until the end of the broadcasting time.

The broadcast ends with all the actors who were on stage during the broadcast taking a bow.

10.1.3.11.6 Contents

Each acting group decides for itself what is to happen on this stage. Sometimes it will be about love, sometimes about hate, and also about at least one of the 18 party themes. The roles are predetermined, but not the distribution and behaviour. Ideas may be exchanged in whispers in the circle. Backstage in the rehearsal room, the ideas are then turned into a play. The audience on the intranet can see backstage and hear what is going to happen, i.e. what the actors are discussing. The show permanently has two broadcast images on the intranet, between which viewers can choose from the intranet. Cameras and directional microphones are installed backstage. The viewer has to decide whether he or she prefers to listen and watch the next team in the pre-show meeting or to follow the play on the other revolving stage. The audience in the studio does not know what will be played.

10.1.3.12 Interactive feature film show

In this show, a feature film is created. Since templates for voting must be filmed by state television, it may be that the production of such a feature film should be direct democracy. Those entitled to vote can use the veto quorum to demand that the feature film be produced in this show. If those entitled to vote consider a feature film that has already been produced to be too biased, they can still use the veto quorum to have it newly produced in that show.

10.1.3.12.1 Genre and screenplay

The show's profile page in the Media Directory serves as a tool to make deciders. As soon as the show is announced, there is a kick-off show in which the concept is introduced and the audience is asked to decide on a genre. Examples are shown for each genre. At the end of the opening show, the genre is decided. If there is a tie or only a 5% difference, the genres are to be combined.

Before the first show, voluntary directors and screenplay writers are asked to submit proposals for screenplays. Ideally, these screenplays already exist. On the show's profile page in the Media Directory, all these proposals are collected and rated by users. The most popular 8 proposals make it into the first broadcast. All authors are invited to the panel and present their story. The audience can ask questions. At the end of the broadcast, either one story is selected from all 8 stories or several stories are combined.

10.1.3.12.2 Directors and actors

Before the second broadcast, directors who would like to film this story apply. To do so, they have to fill out an application form in which they enter their motivation and qualifications and also upload an application video including work samples. The users rate the applicants. The most popular 10 applicants are invited to the show. In the second broadcast, storyboards are created. Directors describe how they would transform the story into sound and vision. Viewers can now decide which director should make the film and which image and sound ideas from other directors should be taken up.

Actors can apply for the roles in the feature film before the third broadcast. They fill out a form on the show's profile page and upload an application video. For the application video, they choose a part from the screenplay and direct it. Also included are older work samples and a personal introduction. The application video may be a maximum of 5 minutes long. Viewers can rate the applicants. The most popular 5 actors per role are invited to the third broadcast. Similar to a casting, all actors now audition for their role. After all applicants have auditioned for a role, the viewers decide which candidate should get the role. At the end of the broadcast, all the roles are cast.

10.1.3.12.3 Locations and filming

In the fourth broadcast, the locations where filming is to take place are selected. For this purpose, the director makes a pre-selection and visits all these locations. He is accompanied by a camera team. In the show, the recordings are shown and compared. The viewers can now vote on which locations should be filmed.

After the fourth broadcast, filming begins and with it the editing. For this purpose, voluntary media designers are needed to edit the video material themselves. All registered media designers will be given access to the video material produced so far and can edit independently on the basis of the storyboard. Admission to the video material of the film is via the profile page of the show in the Media Directory.

In the following broadcasts, reports from the film set are delivered, which the camera team creates, and finished edited film parts are shown. Viewers can now decide which cut to make. After that, this part of the film will no longer be accessible to the voluntary media creators. This will continue until the film is finished. If a part has not been edited satisfactorily, this part will not be blocked.

In the final show, the media designers involved are invited and the whole crew from the film set. The final broadcast is preceded by a screening of the finished film.

11 Nationwide Citizen Television[74]

The Nationwide Citizen Television is a broadcaster by citizens for citizens across the country. Its mission is to present the leisure time of citizens through music, sports, dance, film, culture and art. There is no age limit for citizens' television, children and youths are also allowed to participate and take on any tasks they feel confident in. Party Television supports all amateurs through training, equipment and co-productions.

11.1 Programme

The programme consists of the most popular media content produced by citizens and broadcast and well rated on the Intranet or Local Television. All other programming decisions are made by all users of the Media Directory in the open editorial group for Nationwide Citizen Television. News, documentaries or feature films can be produced by citizens on their own. Feature films can also be co-produced with Party Television.

11.1.1 Shows

The shows are performed by voluntary citizens and are only produced if enough volunteer performers and audience members can be found.

11.1.1.1 Club activities

In this show, unifications present themselves, either in the form of a report on their premises or a presentation of their activities in the studio. A stage set can also be built on which the members of the club then perform a play. This play can also contain improvised parts. For example, volunteers from the audience could be involved to portray new members of the club.

74§184,1,3 Promotion of music, sport, film, culture and art: BV Art.67a, 71

11.1.1.2 Citizen adventures

3 action cameras will be lent to voluntary citizens who have an adventure in mind. The adventurers will be invited to the studio with their shot footage. If they cannot come, they will be asked to comment on their footage with their People's Computer in front of a non-moving background. The broadcast will feature the adventures and the adventurers.

11.1.1.3 People's control

Every week, this show reports and discusses news from politics and the state service. The makers of this broadcast are citizens who, similar to Surveillance Television, visit state enterprises, document them and invite those responsible into the studio. The makers themselves decide on the format. Sometimes it is a talk show, court show, at the office, on the street, privately at home with the focus person or at a pub talk. The show can be recorded in the state enterprises after hours or in a mobile studio.

During controls in state enterprises, the makers are accompanied by at least one policeman. The policeman ensures admission to buildings and rooms as well as the secrecy of protected content. The state employees immediately inform the policeman of the content that needs to be protected so that he can prevent the makers from making recordings of it. The makers, in turn, can ask the Surveillance Television monitoring team to audit this state enterprise and be allowed to be part of the free press during the audit.

11.1.1.4 At home

The show is produced by volunteers in the studio to experience domestic family life in the country. The ministries of family and integration can use this show to simulate family situations and portray subcultures.

The respective living situations are recreated in the studio. There are three stages, two of which are revolving stages. A revolving stage on the left, a rectangular stage in the centre with a desk for the two moderators and another revolving stage on the right. In front of it, the audience is arranged in a semicircle like in an amphitheatre. The moderators are the inhabitants of a flat or a family home in real life. They can be children or adults. Some of their rooms are recreated on stage. Everyday topics that occur in relationships are discussed. Humans who live alone are also included, but they have to express their thoughts. This goes from buying a washing machine to watching the news together. Everyone comments differently. The moderators take turns in the topics. For example, for a couple without children, the male part would have politics, geography, economics and technology. The woman in the couple would, for example, have topics of conversation about sociology, education, culture and sport. These topics are discussed with the partner or friends until one gets bored.

11.1.1.4.1 Pair test

In a couple test, life partners, siblings, parent and child or grandparent and grandchild can test how well they know each other or what they think of each other. To test the characters, tasks are set that are prepared on the filming stages. Tables of contents of daily newspapers are compared to see who likes which sections or articles. From product offers in mailshot advertisements, both make a shopping list and compare the two with each other. Both compare what funny things have already happened or been encountered on the street. Both are supposed to build the ideal room for the other with all their favourite things and then they compare who has the other's tastes better. Both read to each other what they think the other would like.

11.1.1.4.2 Series

As a series, various idiosyncrasies of the residents are presented. In a cooking show, food creations of the residents are shown on the revolving stage in the kitchen and how they are prepared. From healthy cooking to party snacks, everything is included, the main thing is that it is ready in 15 minutes. Clubs introduce themselves that at least one of the residents has visited. Homeless people, drug addicts and subcultures are invited as guests. If it is a resident's birthday, the audience is allowed to join in with games such as jumping rope, sack races, egg races or pot banging. Commercial breaks are made to match the theme of the show. There are food commercials during the 15-minute cooking show. Within a commercial break, there are also videos created by viewers in which commercial clips are made fun of. In the replica flat, products are visibly placed with the logo if the companies pay money for them.

11.1.1.4.3 Outside world

During the show, a balance is to be struck between the studio and the outside world. Switching conversations from the studio to the outside world are represented by a resident talking to a person via video telephony. Video recorded outside is shown on the resident's television or computer. If residents travel, the entire show is done outside the studio using Party Television's fleet of vehicles. At major events such as trade fairs, public festivals, demonstrations, company bankruptcies, in amusement parks, factories, discos, sports competitions that the residents have once attended, the entire show can take place there instead of a video contribution. The prerequisite for this is that the organiser agrees and that the time and opportunity are favourable. The main part of the show could be produced separately in the house or flat instead of on the shooting stages.

11.1.1.4.4 Motto stages

For the revolving stages, there are prefabricated rooms that are subsequently adapted to the respective "residents" by each resident bringing things from their room in the real world to their room on the revolving stage. By default, there are dining room, bedroom, living room, study, kitchen, bathroom, walkway, shop, school, office, hospital and car as motto stages.

12 Surveillance Television[75]

The Surveillance Television is a media control authority. With its monitoring teams, it conducts unannounced searches and undercover investigations in all state institutions at least once a year. The aim of the controls is to check the effectiveness of the state and whether all state organs comply with the laws that apply to them. As a supervisory body, the Surveillance Television is part of the overall supervision of the state.[76] No state organ can invoke secrecy obligations that would prevent control of any area.

The only exceptions are ongoing preliminary investigations and trade secrets that affect the brand essence. Ongoing investigations should not be disturbed by early publication. Therefore, the recordings must be published after the judgement has been pronounced or the preliminary investigation has been discontinued. In the case of trade secrets, the recordings are inspected by the persons affected before publication. Places in the picture or sound that would make trade secrets public are made unrecognisable. It is crucial that cameras are always running and that the monitoring team only edits the recordings in voting with those affected if preliminary investigations or trade secrets are at risk.

The Surveillance Television pays particular attention to the use of taxpayers' money and other state resources in its reporting. The monitoring teams check whether the information provided by a ministry on its revenues and expenditures is accurate. They also control whether the funds are used in accordance with the provisions of the previous budget vote.[77] All state institutions that generate losses that have to be compensated by other parts of the state or the taxpayer are visited as a control body of the financial equalisation system.[78]

---

75 §70,2 Supervision: BV Art.169, §71,4 Review of Effectiveness, §160,1 Financial Supervisory Authority: KV Art.106, §161,4 Financial and Burden Equalisation
76 Ministries of Media, Security, Justice, Finance, State Organisation - 2.1.2.1 Audit services
77 Ministry of Finance - 9.7 Audit Court, 9.5 Budget vote
78 Ministry of Finance - 7.1 Financial and burden equalisation

Special reporting investigates where the losses occur and why. The Surveillance Television has a special responsibility whenever situations are filmed in which citizens are restricted in their fundamental rights or take control of parts in the state. As soon as a city raid, popular empowerment or disaster alert is to be carried out, the Surveillance Television must be alerted as early as possible to document the actions of the state for the citizens as its controllers.

12.1 Monitoring team

The monitoring team walks through the premises of the state institution with cameras and asks questions to the staff. As long as the monitoring team is in the state institution, it has supreme authority to carry out the control. Members of the monitoring team are reporters and cameramen from the Surveillance Television, auditors from the appropriate specialist department in the Company Auditing Agency[79] , an employee from the digital service[80] , police officers[81] , public prosecutors[82] and freelance journalists.

Any media organisation in the Social Market Economy or Free Market Economy and any freelance journalist with a press card can register with the Surveillance Television monitoring team to accompany the controls. Who from the free press accompanies which monitoring team and when is decided by lottery. The free press that has registered to participate in the monitoring team will be put on a waiting list and will participate in turn. Registration is possible with any press card whose issuing association is recognised by the Ministry of Media Affairs and ensures that only full-time journalists receive a press card. The Nationwide Citizen Television also has the right to send free reporters as part of the free press. These freelance reporters do not need a press card, but only need to be registered in the Media Directory as a freelance reporter. The Nationwide Citizen Television has a say in

79 Ministry of Labour - 20.7 Departments of the Company Auditing Agency
80 Ministry of Digital Affairs - 2.1.2.1 Digital Service
81 Ministry of Security - 7 Police
82 Ministry of Justice - 5.6.3 Public Prosecutor's Office

which examinations of state institutions its freelance reporters attend.

12.2 Monitoring trip

For each monitoring trip, two free press film teams consisting of a cameraman and a reporter are allowed to accompany the Surveillance Television monitoring team. The control points are not announced in advance. The monitoring team assembles at a known location and sets off from there to the destination, which is known only to the Surveillance Television reporter until they arrive. During the control, the procedure is similar to a house search, where work has to stop for a short time and all workers are available for questioning. If violations of laws, substandard or unequal services are found during the control, the responsible controllers arrange for further checks by their agency, if necessary, seize evidence and release state employees from service. After the control, the next checkpoint is directly approached. At the end of the monitoring trip, the video footage is turned into reports in the broadcasting centre.

12.3 Programme[83]

The Surveillance Television programme includes reports on nationwide controls in state-owned enterprises, shows on problematic controls, advertisements for success models[84] and for citizen participation in the various control options vis-à-vis the state on the intranet. The news summarises the day's work of all the Surveillance Television's monitoring teams, documentaries show full-length and uncut controls, feature films follow focus persons and shows allow for interactive citizen participation.

---

83 §113.3c Media democracy
84 Ministry of Labour - 20.9 Success Model Directory

12.3.1 News

The Surveillance Television has its daily news, which summarises the reports on the controls made during the day. As special programmes, news is run about a city raid or when the disaster alert has been triggered and the state has to restrict the rights of citizens more than usual.

12.3.1.1 Special broadcast

Special broadcasts are produced as soon as fundamental rights of citizens are restricted by special situations. Special situations such as a city raid, popular empowerment, a disaster caused by humans or nature, or a state of exception, are also subject to designated laws. The Surveillance Television continuously accompanies these special situations with monitoring teams and broadcasts in real time from the places where the events take place.

As soon as the Surveillance Television is alerted by the Ministry of Security, the monitoring teams are immediately contacted. All monitoring teams have already registered in advance in the emergency plans[85] , which are coordinated in advance with the involved authorities and non-state media representatives for various disaster situations.

The monitoring teams are allowed to film anywhere and ask anyone anything. All recordings must first be submitted to the Ministry of Security if, for investigative tactical reasons, a release may only be made in voting with the responsible authorities. If there are no investigative tactics, a release must be made by affected citizens who are clearly identifiable in the recordings. In the case of no release, certain image and sound material is rendered unrecognisable in real time by the image mixers in the control room during reporting. In reports and documentaries, other picture settings are used in which as little as possible had to be made unrecognisable. State employees may not be made unrecognisable except for investigative reasons. Citizens can be made unrecognisable if they want to be. Citizens who are unable to express themselves, for example

---

85Ministry of Security - 5.7.3 Emergency plan

as injured persons in an emergency situation, must be made unidentifiable.

12.3.2 Documentaries

The Surveillance Television broadcasts mainly documentaries consisting of the reports on the monitoring trips and undercover investigations.

12.3.3 Feature films

The Surveillance Television produces feature films by following focus persons biographically. Surveillance Television selects the focus persons itself and can oblige the focus persons to cooperate if the control was very successful or poor. The focal persons can be controllers or controlled. Successful controls are opportunities to find and share a success model. Poor controls are deficiencies that are noticed during the control. Either controllers control poorly or with varying degrees of thoroughness, or controllers raise suspicions of deception or susceptibility to error.

12.3.4 Shows

The shows offer viewers the opportunity to participate in the control of the state and the investigation of failures and violations of the law in the office.

12.3.4.1 Committee of enquiry[86]

The show "Committee of Enquiry" takes place whenever a committee of enquiry is convened.[87] The editorial team can be supported by the editorial teams and staff of the shows "Control Mechanism" and "Covert Investigation". The editorial staff of the show "Control Mechanism" provides the video reports on the violations that led to the committee of enquiry. The

86§97 Investigation Committee: BV Art.153
87Ministry of State Organisation - 12.5.2 Committee of enquiry

editorial staff of the show "Covert Investigation" provides background information on undercover investigations, which, however, may only be shown once the accused has been convicted by a final court decision.

Committees of enquiry are held in the council buildings of the ministries or, if there is a large crowd of the population, in public squares. In the audience are party members of the ruling and opposition party wings. Citizens can participate as spectators through their People's Computers.

Committees of enquiry are basically divided into verdict finding and solution finding. Details of the adjudication process are regulated by the Ministry of Justice[88] . The Ministry of State Organisation is responsible for solution finding and uses the "Solution Finder" show format currently used for legislative committees.

12.3.4.2 Control mechanism

The show "Control Mechanism" deals with all violations that have come out during the controls of the audit services[89] . Violations that are immediately identified by the Surveillance Television monitoring team are investigated while still on site, and the evidence secured and state employees suspended are brought into the show. Voluntary users can view the reports as many times as they like in the Media Directory at any time after they are released on the day of the control. As they do so, they review the footage for possible violations and can report them if necessary. This report is automatically sent to the Federal Moderator's Office and the show's editors. If there is indeed a violation, the affected persons will also be invited to the show. In some cases, it is necessary to be able to prove suspected violations beyond doubt only through undercover investigations. In this case, the editors of the show will wait to invite the affected persons. The editors of the show have the right to conduct their own undercover investigations, which must then be completely uncovered in the following

[88]Ministry of Justice - 5.4.5.2 Committee of enquiry
[89]Ministries of Media, Security, Justice, Finance, State Organisation - 2.1.2.1 Audit services

broadcast.

During the broadcast, together with the viewers, the responsible monitoring team and the responsible state employees, the violations are clarified and how they can be prevented in the future. Also on the panel is the responsible politician in whose area of responsibility the state employees work.

If violations cannot be completely resolved, the people can convene a committee or a committee of enquiry by quorum. A committee is convened whenever a government decision or work instruction is to be taken by the citizens. A committee of enquiry is convened whenever state employees are alleged to have committed criminal offences.

As a regular feature, the show reviews the impact of new laws after 2, 10 and 25 years. If there has been an unintended impact, viewers can voice it here and call for a vote for the repeal quorum of the law.

12.3.4.3 Covert investigation

This show takes place when, after undercover investigations of politicians, a committee of enquiry and court proceedings were initiated that ended in a guilty verdict.[90]

Potentially criminal politicians are observed and questioned by undercover investigators from their environment. The undercover investigators are employees of the Ministry of Security who document their investigations by video. The recordings are forwarded to the show's editorial team. Once the undercover investigations are completed, all investigations and court proceedings are followed by a camera crew from the show. If a guilty verdict is reached, all participants, defendants, politicians and judges as well as all senior police officers, prosecutors, lawyers, judges and lay judges will be invited to the show to answer questions from viewers. If the criminal politicians have been sentenced to imprisonment, they will be given supervised furlough for the visit to the broadcast or will be connected via video telephony.

The show consists of a documentary film edited together from the undercover and non-undercover investigations as well

---

90 Ministry of State Organisation - 12.5.2 Committee of enquiry

as the court proceedings. This is followed by the discussion panel in the show. The aim of the discussion is to find out what has become of the proposals for measures made in the show "Control Mechanism", in the committee or committee of enquiry because of the incident.

12.3.4.4 Real-time monitoring

This broadcast is intended to create complete transparency in the state service, if necessary. As soon as state institutions are suspected of corruption, citizens can report it. The Surveillance Television investigates the suspicion of corruption and can obtain an order for real-time surveillance from the responsible public prosecutor's office at the National Court of Justice. Real-time surveillances are limited to one week. They can only be ordered by a judge of the National Court of Justice for a longer period. Citizens can, in the event of a reported suspicion of corruption and subsequent inaction by state authorities, open a veto quorum for the case and, after a majority vote, order real-time surveillance.
Affected state service workers will then be required to wear a 360° camera while at work, which will transmit their image in real time to the Beta channel of the Surveillance Television. In addition, a remote-controlled camera that can be moved along two axes will be set up in the affected rooms of state institutions. Viewers can control these remotely via the intranet, i.e. rotate and focus.

12.3.4.5 Critical reflection on broadcasts

This show is about the comments that arise during and after the consumption of a broadcast in the Media Directory. This show will feature the clips of the broadcast and the related comments with the most views, best ratings or most critical questions. Affected politicians, makers of the affected broadcast, and authors of popular comments, are invited to the show for a panel discussion to discuss the comments.

12.3.4.6 Researched

In this show, the topics from the previous week's news are newly investigated with primary sources. No copying from other media is allowed. Every day, the previous day's news is reviewed and interviews are conducted one day later. Once a week, this show runs on Surveillance Television and presents all the findings that have been forgotten or misrepresented by other media. What was forgotten, the reporters discover in their investigations. What was misrepresented is told to them by affected people who were reported on and who accordingly followed these video clips with indignation. Affected people and editors or reporters from the relevant media are invited into the studio for the show. Employees of the state media must appear on the show.

12.3.4.7 Advertising test

During the show, commercials are shown. After the commercial break, the first and last product from the commercial is tested in the studio. The audience is also allowed to try out the product and vote on it. Guests in the studio are technical auditors from the Company Auditing Agency who bring test equipment or have already tested the product in their laboratories.

12.3.4.8 Brussels lace

In this show, the politicians of the European Union are rated. Domestic citizens are interviewed about what they don't like about European Union policies. Citizens are asked questions on the Vox pop boxes about what they think of the European Union or certain European Union regulations or directives. Amusingly pointed passages from the video contributions or the discussion in the forum on the show's profile page in the Media Directory are re-voiced by a team of actors in the studio during the show. Affected politicians are invited to the studio and can comment on the ratings. Responsible Ministry of Foreign Affairs officials must come to the broadcast and cannot decline the invitation.

13 Educational Television[91]

The Educational Television is a broadcaster for education and research. The content is co-produced with companies, research institutions and educational institutions. The filming schedules are derived from the curricula of the educational institutions[92] , from the training plans of the companies[93] as well as from the annual accountability report of the Company Auditing Agency[94] , success models[95] and the latest research results from research projects[96] .

Companies in Planned Economy and Social Market Economy and state educational institutions are obliged to co-produce, companies and educational institutions in Free Market Economy can report voluntarily.

The task of this broadcaster is to make written, applied and researched knowledge accessible in multimedia form with different formats, such as feature films, PC games, radio plays or animations. First, all the literature that is necessary to pass all state educational qualifications will be filmed. Finally, an archive of knowledge will be built that covers everything from nursery school to professor and will be regularly updated.

13.1 Cooperation with educational institutions

The Educational Television works with the Examinations Office[97] to produce examinations for performance records submitted by examinees as videos. In consultation with the Examinations Office, the Educational Television creates suitable screenplays that serve as the assignment of tasks for

---

91 §182,1,2 Further education: BV Art. 64a
92 Ministry of Education - 5.10.9.1 Curriculum implementation, 8.7.4 Subjects, 9.15 School subjects
93 Ministry of Education - 11.3 Vocational training college, 11.6.8 Higher education degrees
94 Ministry of Labour - 20.4 Accountability Report
95 Ministry of Labour - 20.9 Success Model Directory
96 Ministry of Innovation - 5.3 Research Directory, 5.4 State research projects
97 Ministry of Education - 4.6 Examinations Office

the performance record. As long as all examinees follow the same screenplay and only film excerpts from it in a division of labour, the viewer can follow the plot more easily later on. The Educational Television works with the Education Authority to develop film projects with teachers for project teaching that fit the curriculum and the Educational Television's programme.[98] Film projects can also follow a common screenplay across the country, based on a division of labour.

In this way, extensive film projects can be filmed in a division of labour. It is up to the Educational Television editors to choose the type of cooperation. The learners, teachers and researchers can organise themselves via the Education Directory and determine the actions of the editorial teams in a committee by means of a veto quorum.

13.2 Programme[99]

The Educational Television's programme consists of learning content from teaching at state educational institutions, filming of scientific literature, the latest research results and successful production methods. To produce the programme, the Educational Television makes use of the Government Television and Party Television fleets and studios. In addition, the Educational Television has mobile homes with camera equipment and video editing suites that are parked in the company car park, school yard or campus as long as filming is taking place there. The Educational Television's broadcast centre is located in the Ministry of Education's capital city.

13.2.1 News

The Educational Television news programme reports weekly on the latest research from state schools, colleges, universities, institutes and around the world. The editors of the Educational Television work together with the scientists of the Ministry

98 Ministry of Education - 4.5 Education Authority, 5.12.1.2 Project teaching
99 §113.3d Media democracy

of Education. The editors share the work with the scientists. No matter who has read a new article, they rate it in the Education Directory. Entries that are important to society as a whole are automatically sent by link in a message to the Educational Television's profile in the Media Directory. The aim is to filter out the published texts from scientific journals according to their importance for the people as a whole and to film them in video clips. In this news programme, great importance is attached to the fact that the sources are inserted behind a contribution and are linked to a time stamp in the contribution. This makes it easy for other Educational Television broadcasts, other broadcasters or interested citizens to look up the sources on which the feature is based. The sources can be used to make a film, a new research project, a suggestion for improvement or a new idea.

13.2.1.1 News from the research

All state research projects are regularly visited by Educational Television. The latest findings of the individual scientific fields in the state universities are filmed and broadcast as video clips. The Educational Television does not necessarily only produce at domestic universities, but may also film research results from foreign countries by invitation. The sources for each contribution can be called up in the teletext or in the Media Directory.
New knowledge gained in colleges is filmed by the subject area in student performance records. The performance records with the best rating are sent to the newsroom.

13.2.2 Documentaries

The documentaries reflect knowledge from the subject areas. They can have elements of a feature film, but remain documentary films that depict knowledge truthfully.

13.2.2.1 Learning content for degrees

All state educational institutions use the Educational Television to film their teaching content, which is required for all degrees.[100] Educational Television mobile camera teams visit the teachers with the best ratings and the classes and courses with the best average grades in a subject throughout the country. All teams collectively cover all subjects and learning years. In the first round, the teams film in documentary format. The following rounds are possible in show and feature film formats and are co-produced with the classes or courses. Educational Television film crews visit classes until the entire curriculum taught is filmed at all primary, comprehensive and, colleges. Then each subject is edited together. National language and maths would be the longest films because they are already in primary school and both subjects can be studied. These become pure documentaries of the curriculum of all degrees based on video recordings from lessons.

All visual material is published in the Knowledge Directory[101] and can be rated by users. This helps to identify the most popular teachers. There, a film crew newly comes by and films even more of the lessons, if possible everything the popular teacher has to offer.

The Knowledge Directory algorithm can, if the user selects the setting, display videos that are most accessible to the user based on all their own profile data. Since there are many videos in the Knowledge Directory, the type of learner and the presentation of the learning content is crucial. Funny people, for example, like it when knowledge is presented in an amusing way. Well-read professionals like technical terms and complex points of view. Authors, for their part, give their works keywords that say how the knowledge is presented. Users can rate these keywords as accurate or inaccurate and also assign keywords themselves.

---

100 Ministry of Education - 12.4 Digitised education
101 Ministry of Education - 12.7 Knowledge Directory

13.2.2.2 Knowledge Filmmaker

The documentary "Knowledge Filmmakers" is produced as a series. The aim is to film the production process of all formats broadcast on state television and available in the Knowledge Directory.

Each episode is set in a different age group in a different school subject. Each season it is the turn of a different format, i.e. documentary, feature film, reportage, music video or show. With this documentary, it becomes clear how the respective format is produced. However, it is not only about the techniques of filmmaking, but especially about how to make films out of scientific content. Here, the special source work is shown that proves the correctness of learning content.

The documentary is produced by a film team from the Educational Television, which travels to the various filming locations in a caravan. The film team accompanies selected film productions at primary, comprehensive and higher education institutions.

In order to document independently produced learning videos of users in the Knowledge Directory, the most popular learning videos are collected and all authors of the most popular learning videos are asked. Editors ask the authors if they are willing to produce a new video in the same way and be filmed doing it. At the end of the episode, the learning video whose production process was documented is shown.

13.2.2.3 Good corporate governance

Positive and negative examples of entrepreneurial activity are shown by the Company Auditing Agency. The Educational Television investigates successful production methods in the Success Model Directory[102] and films their introduction in affected companies. The Company Auditing Agency provides a report to the Educational Television every year. This report contains examples of successful or unsuccessful business management. In the listing per sector, care is taken to digitally extract the most frequent faults and the most frequent correct

---

102Ministry of Labour - 20.9 Success Model Directory

decisions from the entire audit reports of all companies. The names of the individual companies are only listed if the companies have agreed and want to advertise in this way. If the companies have not agreed, company names are invented. Innovative production methods and patent products can also be classified as "secret" by the companies and are not filmed. The Company Auditing Agency anonymises the data, except for contact details, so that the editors can ask affected companies for access rights. The more efficient solution or the negative example is filmed in an imaginary company as long as no company agrees to documentary filming.

13.2.2.4 Economic cycles

This film is about how value creation works in the four different economic forms. There are many ways to get the goods that are produced and freely sold in the different economic forms. The value chain of the products is shown here and how buyers can buy socially or efficiently. At the end, the money cycle of the two currencies of Social Market Economy and Free Market Economy, the working hours in the Social Market Economy and the barter transactions in the Barter Economy will be made clear. It should become apparent that by buying a product from an economic form, one also supports this system. Unless one works in this system oneself, one could also damage oneself through one's purchase.

13.2.2.5 Money life

This documentary is produced as an animated film. It takes the first-person perspective of a banknote. It runs through the real economy and the digital economy. At the beginning, the banknote is produced, stored, distributed by the Note-issuing Bank to the banks and dispensed via an ATM. In the real economy, it spends time in wallets, cash registers and ATMs. Once deposited into the bank account, it begins its digital journey around the world across all asset classes of the stock market, from stocks and bonds to commodities, currencies and bets. It experiences rising and falling prices, thus gaining and losing further companions as money notes. After the stock market period, the banknote returns to the real economy. Depending on the economic situation, it is now worth more or less, which becomes clear as soon as it is exchanged for a high-value or low-value product. To illustrate inflation and deflation, the journey between the real economy and the finance economy is repeated. In the end, the banknote is taken to the Central Bank by an armoured car company and destroyed. In the obituary, its age is mentioned and how much value it has lost or gained through inflation or deflation in the course of its existence.

13.2.2.6 Videowiki

In the Videowiki, things are explained with a video. The structure is like Wikipedia, only with videos instead of text. The video clips are cut so that each clip is there for one article. The start screen of the video shows the table of contents of the article. If you click on a subheading, the playback jumps immediately to that point in the video. The video is in the middle of the page view. Above it is the title, to the left of it is the video's table of contents, to the right of it are all the links to the video, arranged chronologically from top to bottom. The links to other videos in which certain terms are explained are also displayed in the timeline.

13.2.3 Feature films

13.2.3.1 Textbook filming

The Educational Television, in cooperation with the teaching educational institutions, ensures the filming of textbooks used there. Priority is given to all textbooks of which most of the content appears in the examinations for state educational qualifications. All educational institutions using the same textbook will participate in the filming. The filming is divided into the chapters of the textbook and distributed to the learners as assignments. Whether these tasks are done in class or a performance record is left up to the teachers and learners. All the edited parts of the film and all the video material is sent to the Educational Television, where it is edited together, broadcast and stored in the Knowledge Directory.

13.2.4 Shows

In the shows, education and research content is filmed in cooperation with teachers, learners and researchers.

13.2.4.1 Presentation

People can give a ten-minute presentation in the show using any media, such as screen presentations. The speakers propose the topic on the show's profile page in the Media Directory and users can rate the topic proposals. The topic with the most positive votes will be included in the broadcast.

13.2.4.2 Who will be a teacher?

At state educational institutions, curricula and educational literature are filmed. All examinees who deliver a performance record as a video and all teaching courses that submit a finished film project automatically take part in the casting for the show "Who wants to be a teacher? In the show, the 10 funniest, most understandable and most correct videos will be chosen, each in its own category. The categories "Funny" and "Understandable" are awarded by the users regardless of the grade. The "Correct" category is awarded by the teachers with the grade. Excerpts of the videos are shown in the broadcast and the makers of the videos are invited to the show.

13.2.4.3 Innovation Lab

This show is produced on a mobile or stationary basis, depending on the topic. It is the media accompaniment to state research projects.[103] The Ministry of Innovation operates mobile Innovation Labs to jointly work out pressing questions of the economy for technical progress as a people. For this purpose, the trucks with the mobile Innovation Labs tour the country. Each mobile lab is equipped differently and requires prior knowledge in handling the substances and devices present in the lab. This is where the show comes in. The show provides the necessary education and networking for the voluntary researchers. At the beginning of a tour with new experimental materials, all materials, such as devices and substances, are explained and put into different known experimental arrangements that can have dangerous consequences. Special attention is given to warnings and how to protect oneself when handling certain materials.

All mobile Innovation Labs are equipped with cameras for security reasons. These cameras are television cameras with microphones. The best recordings are edited together for a show. As soon as the lab director recognises an innovation, he announces it. The inventor or inventors are then asked to speak into a designated camera in the lab to introduce themselves. All inventors are invited to the show, as well as company representatives who could make money from this innovation. In addition, auditors from the Company Auditing Agency and the Innovation Agency[104] are regular guests in the studio. The aim of the discussion on the panel is to get an innovation ready for the market.

---

103 Ministry of Innovation - 6.5 Mobile Innovation Labs, 5.4 State Research Projects
104 Ministry of Innovation - 4 Innovation Agency

14 Youth Television[105]

The Youth Television broadcasts appropriate content for children aged 6 to 18 at the appropriate times. Children under 6 should not watch television at all, but discover the natural world. The mission of the Youth Television is to give children and youths the admission to information that adults also receive, albeit to a different extent. The broadcaster's content mostly deals with the ministries of education and family, for which youths as young as ten years old are entitled to vote. In addition, adolescents have increased information needs regarding all the changes in their bodies and ways of thinking, which the Youth Television covers.

14.1 Production

The broadcasting centre is located in the capital city of the Ministry of Family Affairs. The production of the Youth Television content is done by Youth Television workers, sometimes in cooperation with other ministries and minors. Teachers at the educational institutions support the Youth Television staff in preparing content from the other state broadcasters in a child-friendly way and adapting it to the learning level.

Third-party productions are also possible if minors send in contributions, as adults can do through Citizen Television. Purchases are the exception and are only approved for old children's films that have shaped generations.

The children and youths produce news, documentaries, feature films and shows on their own initiative, as part of a mentoring programme or in class. To support the amateurs in production, Youth Television media educators travel to educational institutions or youth centres and teach the adolescents how to operate the equipment they bring along themselves. The entire film project is designed democratically.[106] Depending on the format and scope, an entire educational institution can be involved in the production, Youth Television camera teams

---

105§184,1,3 Promotion of music, sport, film, culture and art: BV Art.67a, 71
106Ministry of Education - 8.8.3.1.1 Project example: Producing a film

can be requested and the vehicle fleet or film and television studios of the state broadcasting authorities can be used. The content is determined by the minors and checked by the Youth Television editors for protection of minors.

14.2 Rating

All videos voluntarily produced by minors over the age of ten can be uploaded to the Media Directory via their People's Computer. All productions from educational institutions are rated by the entire educational institution where they were produced and, if they receive a good rating, are released for public viewing in the Media Directory. All these productions can be rated by viewers via the intranet. The productions with the best ratings run in the Youth Television's programme and, if they work scientifically and present knowledge, are also included in the Knowledge Directory. At the annual domestic children's and youths' film festival, the 50 most popular films by minors are rated by the entire audience and the winner is given a role as director or actor in a state film production of his or her election.

14.3 Programme

The Youth Television programme includes news programmes, documentaries, feature films and shows. The broadcasts alternate between programmes produced by Youth Television staff, programmes produced by minors themselves, programmes co-produced by minors and Youth Television, and programmes produced by educational institutions.

14.3.1 News

In the news programme, good news is disseminated and bad news from the general news programmes is explained and put into an understandable context.

14.3.1.1 Child-friendly advertising

Instead of advertising, learning videos from the Knowledge Directory are shown. Depending on the time of broadcast or the audience ratings of a particular target group, the learning content is adapted to the learning level of the target group.

14.3.1.2 Federal punch

In the broadcast, all the ministries' press conferences per week are translated into a puppet show. The puppets play in front of a screen on which the matching background is superimposed. The puppet theatre is played with matching play figures. Each puppet represents a ministry or a politician. For example, the crocodile would be there for the health ministry. Everything that the Ministry of Health does, the crocodiles do together. For example, all crocodiles could have health insurance. Punch represents the Federal Moderator and provides funny moments in his role.

14.3.2 Documentaries

The Youth Television produces documentaries in cooperation with the viewers or with the ministries of family and education. Minor viewers can document things that are important to them with the camera and send them in. The ministries of education and family explain the rights and duties of minors in documentaries and provide information about the physical and mental developments of adolescents.

14.3.2.1 Childhood and youth

The documentary is produced as a series. Each season will feature different activities and states of mind, with different age groups featured in the episodes.
Voluntary children and youths can keep a video diary and send their videos to the show's editorial team. They can include interests, leisure activities, feelings, thoughts, friends,

love partners, parents or siblings. In the editorial office, the videos are edited together and sent to the authors and parents for review and approval. The aim is to show a progression over years by asking the same questions newly every 3 years and keeping a video diary. How many days the video diary is kept is up to the authors. It is only intended to answer the questions via video and to describe activities or states of mind. Individual documentaries are produced once someone has sent in video diaries over at least 15 years. This person will be visited by a camera crew once they are of age of majority and a party will be held for the film, attended by all participants.

14.3.3 Feature films

Feature films can be created or purchased based on the imagination of the children watching. The acquisitions are intended to help connect the generations. Old children's series and films from all over Europe such as "Once upon a time there was a human being", knowledge shows such as "The Mouse Show", documentaries such as "Dandelion", feature films such as "Emil and the Detectives" are included in the programme.

14.3.3.1 Fairy tales by the fireside

The moderator or skilled reader reads out old fairy tales. He sits in a wing chair next to a fireplace so that the fire can be watched while the story is being read. If there are several roles in the fairy tale, all the speakers of the roles sit together on one or two sofas.

14.3.3.2 Bag of tricks

The primary schools jointly produce an animated film in co-production with Youth Television. The screenplay is created by all participating classes executing the first steps of the film production project.[107] Each primary school has a

---

107 Ministry of Education - 8.8.3.1.1 Project example: Producing a film

photo box for depicting scenes using drawings or toys. The filming of an animated film is very time-consuming with 25 frames per second and 1500 frames per minute. Therefore, the clips per class should be as short as possible. Each primary school produces an excerpt from the screenplay and sends it to Youth Television. At the broadcasting centre, the clippings are put together to make the finished film. The film is shown on Youth Television during the summer holidays.

14.3.3.3 Virtue filming

This series is about the good virtues that make life communal. Proverbs, qualities like punctuality, charity, accuracy and honesty are filmed. The stories are told with non-human creatures. Animals and plants behave virtuously, express it very honestly and praise each other for it when they notice it in the other. Those who do not observe virtues are valued less, despised or hunted by the other animals and plants.
This feature film is produced as an animated series. The episodes consist of examples of different virtues. The seasons consist of virtues, norms, values, traditions, philosophies and beliefs.

14.3.4 Shows

The shows offer children their first experience of interactive co-determination and youths the opportunity to influence their television programme.

14.3.4.1 Who does not ask remains stupid

In this show, questions are collected from children aged 3 to 18 and answered in experiments or explorations. Children can send in the questions, or perplexed parents who have been asked a question by their child. The questions are sorted by frequency, answered in the show and saved as a video file in the Knowledge Directory.
For children, there is also the possibility to personally ask all

the persons appearing in Youth Television something. Every child can write their question in the comments under the video in the Media Directory, just like any other user. In the case of children, the question is automatically sent to the editors. If questions pile up for a person, that person will be invited to be a guest on the show. Children whose question is selected are also invited to the show. During the show, the invited children interview and talk to the guest first, then the audience. The audience for this show consists exclusively of children.

14.3.4.2 Flirtwalk

This show is about turning unmated persons into couples. The Ministry of Family Affairs supports the show by organising such events all over the country.[108]
All candidates and guests in the audience must apply to take part in the show. To do so, they fill out a questionnaire on the show's profile page in the Media Directory. An algorithm selects candidates and audience guests who match each other. Accordingly, focal points are set in each individual broadcast. Should a sufficient number of interested parties be looking for the same age groups, genders and preferences, candidates and audience guests are selected accordingly. For example, persons looking for persons from the age group between 50 and 60 can be invited in one broadcast.

14.3.4.2.1 Candidates

The candidates also apply with a 1-minute video. Other users can watch these videos and vote for the candidates. Anyone who has applied to take part in the show and votes for a candidate is automatically recorded if both have enough in common. The algorithm tries to invite both to the same show if possible. The candidates with the most votes are invited to the show. With all these candidates, 5-minute introduction videos are produced in advance by a camera team.

---

108 Ministry of Family Affairs - 7.3 Partnering

14.3.4.2.2 Audience

Only unmated persons are admitted as audience and care is taken to ensure that about as many male as female guests are admitted and that their interests are similar. For the different preferences asked for in the questionnaire, there are different seating compartments in the grandstand, for example for heterosexuals, homosexuals, sapiosexuals, poliamoureuses or dominants.

14.3.4.2.3 Business cards

Photo booths are set up in the entrance area of the grandstand, where you can create 100 business cards. Printed on the front is the picture, name, telephone number and addresses of internet and intranet profiles, email and postcode. Candidates and public guests can make business cards here in advance to exchange with all candidates or public guests of their choice.

14.3.4.2.4 Relationship or sex

On the business cards, the right short side is coloured yellow, the left blue. Those who only want sex or a relationship can tear in or tear off the corresponding side. At the skating exhibition, applicants who only want sex or only a relationship wear a corresponding bracelet or necklace. Blue means relationship, yellow means sex. Candidates must already express this preference in their interview video or decide on a case-by-case basis. The individual case decision must be expressed in the backstage get-to-know-you interview.

14.3.4.2.5 Merge

In the show, there are two doors in a wall on the stage that lead backstage. In the door frame there are red lamps on the outer side and green lamps on the central side. A letterbox is mounted next to each door. Behind the doors the candidates gather, men behind the left door, women behind the right door. Homosexual candidates line up with the opposite sex. The doors are transparent mirrors on one side. The mirrored side faces the audience. Next to each door are two vents with fans on the right and left. The fans move the air in front of the door behind the door so that candidates can smell their applicants.

Volunteers from the audience line up for the candidate(s) of their choice. As soon as a candidate is announced, applicants can line up until 30 applicants have been allowed to skate in front of a candidate. Audience members may also line up more than once.

Two queues form 10 metres in front of the doors. Here, the men queue on the right and the women queue on the left. Anyone who jumps the queue is no longer allowed to queue. Persons who have queued but are no longer allowed to do so can drop their business card in the letterbox next to the door. The letterbox will be emptied before the next candidate behind that door takes their turn. These business cards will be given to the respective candidate after the show.

14.3.4.2.6 Procedure

At the beginning, the first candidate steps behind the left door. The moderator announces him and shows the 1 minute and 5 minute introduction video.

Now the first applicant in line starts walking towards the mirrored door. He sees himself, can make a pantomime gesture and also say something. He can shape the 10 metres he walks towards the mirror as he likes. As soon as he arrives in front of the mirror, the candidate presses the red or green button behind the door to activate the corresponding lights. Each candidate has a maximum of 30 seconds to do this, but at least 10 seconds to look the applicant, who is standing directly in front of the mirror, in the eye.

Each candidate is allowed to send a maximum of 10 applicants backstage through the green light. Once the candidate has been allowed to see all the applicants from their skating exhibition queue, they come through the mirrored door and go backstage.

Behind the stage there are rooms for getting to know each other and a lounge. In the get-to-know rooms there are cameras, microphones, two chairs and a table. In the common room there is a seating area and a bar. Each candidate goes into a get-to-know room and all applicants go into the lounge. Assistants from the show bring new applicants into the get-to-know rooms every minute.

Each candidate gets to know each applicant in a 1-minute interview. After 10 minutes, he or she must choose one, several or no applicants. If more than one applicant is selected, they can decide whether or not to engage in a group relationship or group sex. Candidates who have not selected an applicant, as well as spurned applicants, sit back down in the audience and are allowed to queue with more candidates. Fresh couples are allowed to take a seat on a sofa in the box. Their one-minute get-to-know-you session is edited together by the director and shown in the broadcast after all candidates have had their turn. Now it is the turn of the next candidate of the opposite sex behind the right-hand door and he or she can again choose 10 applicants from a maximum of 30. After no more candidates are behind the doors, the show draws to a close. Now all the fresh couples are interviewed and the one-minute conversation of the two is shown as a video.

14.3.4.3 SOS Singles On Stage

The show runs in the evening programme and is recorded in different locations. The logo of the show is a white heart with a red cross in the middle. The show is held either with a mobile studio or in a studio building. The profile page for the show in the Media Directory gives the locations and dates.
Couples who have met on one of these shows are asked to tell the editorial team when they have married or had a child. At the end of the broadcast, the moderator announces the happy embassies.

14.3.4.3.1 Mobile

The mobile event takes place in places where enough unmated persons stay for a sufficiently long time. This can be, for example, in an open-air swimming pool, a pedestrian zone, a hotel, amusement park, circus, cinema, fitness studio or on a camping site. It is crucial that there is enough space for the mobile studio and that the operators have permission. The operators are approached by the editors or apply to the editors. The show team distributes flyers at the location to unmated persons who have time to flirt for one hour. The distribution happens after the mobile studio is set up and lasts one hour. After that, all the volunteers gather and the show begins.

14.3.4.3.2 Stationary

For a stationary event, a studio with a stage and an audience is needed. Only unmated persons who also want to participate are allowed in the audience. They can sign up on the show's profile page in the Media Directory. There is the option to wait for postcode areas. So that unmated persons from all over the country can participate in a meaningful way, registrations are collected from postcode areas. For example, in one week the audience would be predominantly singles who come from a 200 kilometre radius around the city of Kiel. Depending on how many singles have registered from an area, the radius becomes larger or smaller. The stationary show is recorded in various film studios around the country so that long journeys from corresponding postcode areas are not necessary.

14.3.4.3.3 Procedure

All those present stand in a circle and three getting-to-know-you games are played. Through these games, the names and characteristics of the participants are introduced. This is followed by two acting improvisations. In the first play, two participants each are given a situation from which they spontaneously start acting on stage. The situations are different family relationship conflicts and each of the two participants is given a role as a family member. In the second play, 5 persons are given one role, the so-called focus person. One participant takes on this role and all the other group members think of roles that have to do with this focus person. The group is given 30 minutes to think up a situation, distribute the roles and change clothes. Then they act out their situation on stage. After the play, the audience is asked to vote by show of hands who the focus person was. To do this, everyone from a group lines up and steps in front of the audience one after the other. After getting to know each other and acting, all the blindfolded men are put on stage and put bowls behind them with slips of paper with the same number. The women take a slip of paper from each man in the bowl that they like. Afterwards, the men take off their blindfolds and are told their number. The women are blindfolded and placed on the stage. On the back of their chairs, the slips of paper with the numbers they had previously chosen are visibly displayed on the floor. The men look for where their number can be found. Men who have been selected more than once have to choose a woman to stand by. A countdown of 360 seconds is counted down. If several men are standing in front of the same woman, they can still stand by another woman who has chosen them. The moderator finishes by saying, "You'll see if you're really standing right when your eyes open." Then the women are allowed to take off their blindfolds. If there are several men standing in front of her, she can choose one or all of them. If she chooses all of them, all those men who do not want a group relationship can leave.

15 Switching to the new system

The Ministry of Media Affairs is being rebuilt to represent the fourth state powers, the mediative, alongside the Ministry of Digital Affairs. Funding is provided through tax money, paid-for commissioned productions from companies and advertising. Tax money is distributed through the budget vote and is earmarked for constitutional tasks of the mediative. Additional revenues are used for more elaborate productions or acquisitions.

15.1 Restructuring of the broadcasters

The state regional broadcasting authorities with their radio and TV channels are taken over by the Government Television, Local Television and News Television. The Government Television moves its production to the existing broadcasting centres of the state regional broadcasters, which are mostly located in the capital cities of the regions, as these capital cities will later become the capital cities of the ministries. Regional state broadcasters take over from the Local Television. Missing broadcasting centres are gradually established, but if there is sufficient capacity in the remaining broadcasting centres, they may consist of only one office in the town hall.

All other domestic and foreign offices of the state media are merged and duplications in one city or foreign country are closed.

The Party Television takes over the nationwide state broadcasting authorities. The broadcasting centre is expanded and all other field offices are moved to the broadcasting centres in the capital cities.

Surveillance Television takes over a government broadcaster and some of its personnel from domestic and foreign secret services.

The Educational Television takes over state foreign broadcasters and the personnel for documentaries and reports.

The Youth Television takes over the state broadcasters for children and youths.

Civic Television from the Local Television and Party Television takes over all open channels in the country.

The state radio stations are either closed or converted. Only so many radio stations will be retained that as many state radio stations as state TV channels can be received. The regional radio stations will be preserved to the extent that one radio station will be in charge of regional television. All foreign offices of the radio stations will be closed.

15.2 Conversion of the old ministries

All departments and units that transfer to the Ministry of Media Affairs are listed below. If only the department or sub-department is named, all its units are taken over. If individual units are named, only those units are transferred. All departments and units not named are dropped. Existing staff adapt their tasks to the new requirements. The corresponding names of the units can usually be found as keywords in the running text.

15.2.1 Foreign Office[109]

E European Department
European political public relations

15.2.2 Federal Ministry of Justice and Consumer Protection[110]

III Trade and Commercial Law
Media law

15.2.3 All ministries

Quality management, evaluation, prevention of corruption, protection against sabotage, disciplinary matters, press and public relations, civil dialogue, minister's spokesperson, speeches and texts, conferences, events

---

109 https://www.auswaertiges-amt.de/blob/215270/004ca2ab6cbacdd63 78eee0eb8077417/organisationsplan-data.pdf Status: 17.05.2019
110 https://www.bmjv.de/SharedDocs/Downloads/DE/Ministerium/ Organisationsplan/Organisationsplan_DE.pdf;jsessionid=A807B5B1F5E FC74825E8B2A6508405BE.2_cid297?__blob=publicationFile&v=131 Viewed on: 14/05/2019

Contact form

Dear reader

If you would like to make what you have read come true, in whole or in part, together with other like-minded people, I offer you several possibilities with this contact form. Fill it out, tear out the page and send it by post to:

Andreas Seidl, P.O. Box 1206, 63488 Seligenstadt / Germany

Or send the details to:

Phone: 0049 1522 818 2243 (whatsapp, telegram, signal)

Email: andreas.seidl2022@web.de

Please mark with a cross:

O   I want to found a dynamic People's Party.

O   I want to donate money for implementation.

O   I want contacts with like-minded people in my area.

Forename: _______________________________________

Surname: _______________________________________

Please fill in only the contact option through which a reply should be made.

Street, house no.:   _______________________________

Postcode, city, country: _______________________________

Phone: _______________________________

Email address: _______________________________